FLOWER FOR STRESS RELIEVING

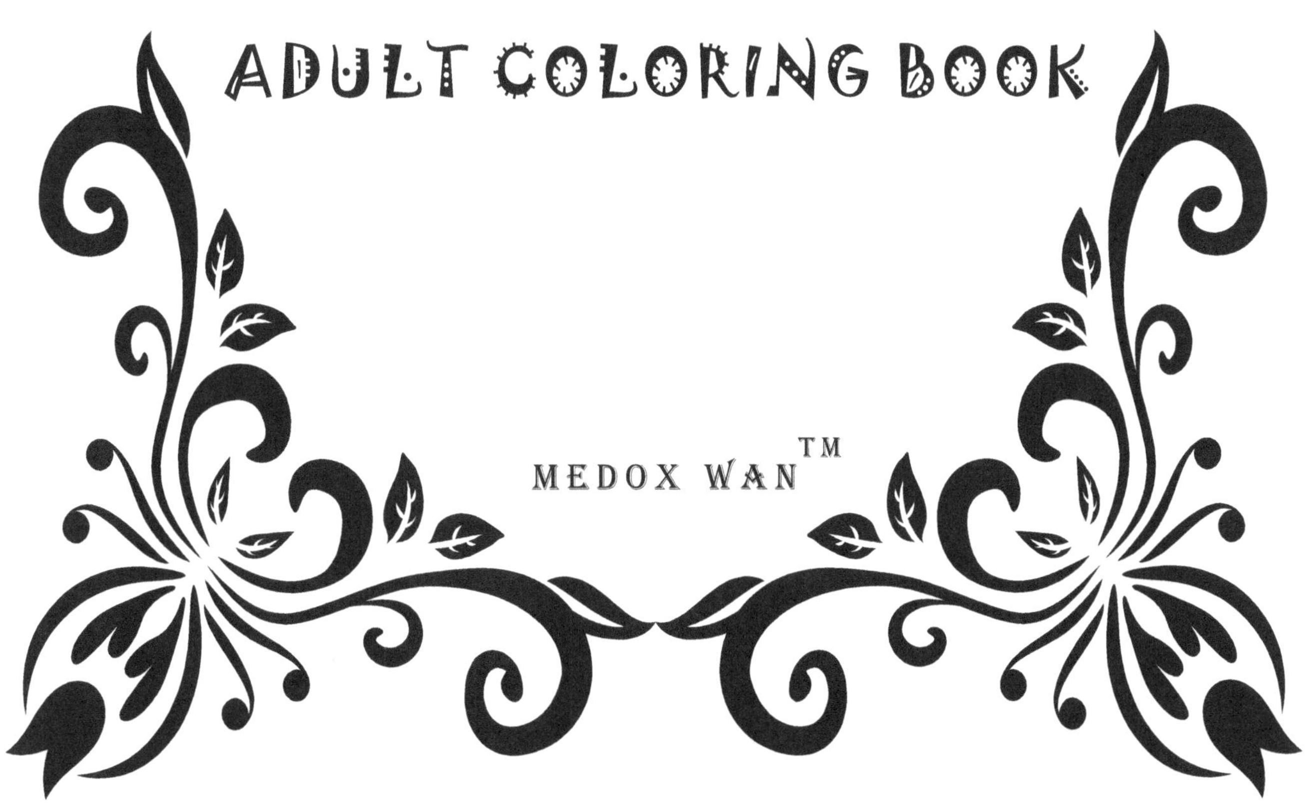

ADULT COLORING BOOK

MEDOX WAN™

THIS BOOK BELONGS TO:

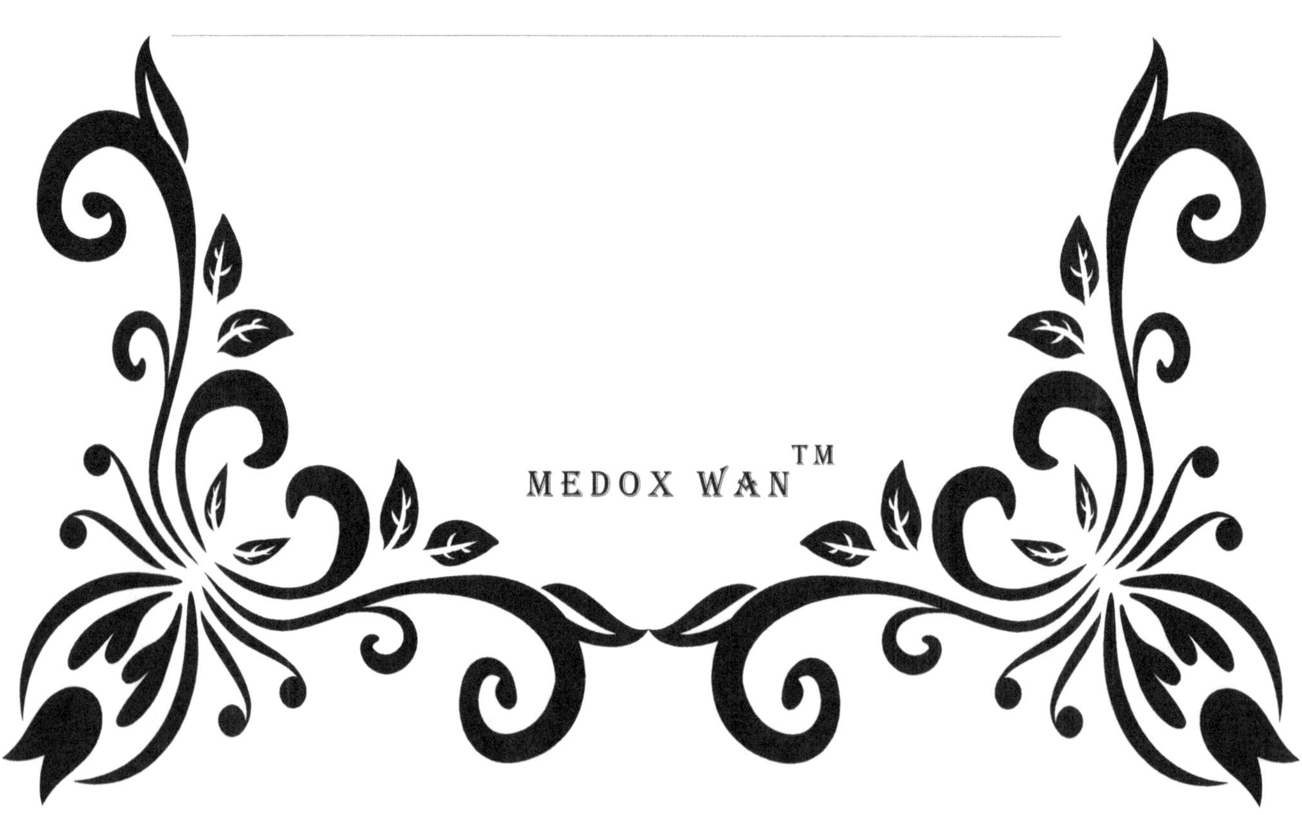

MEDOX WAN™

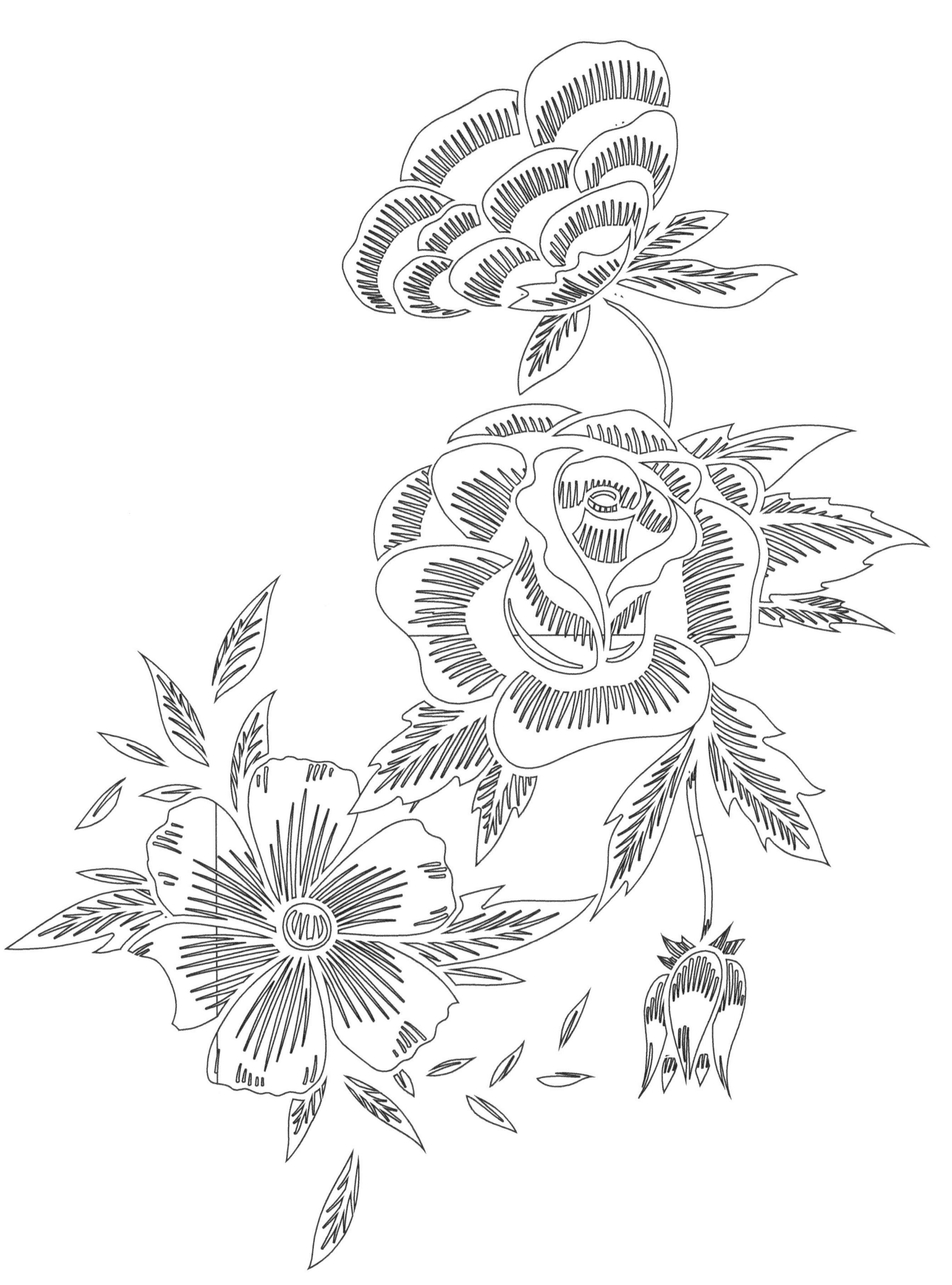

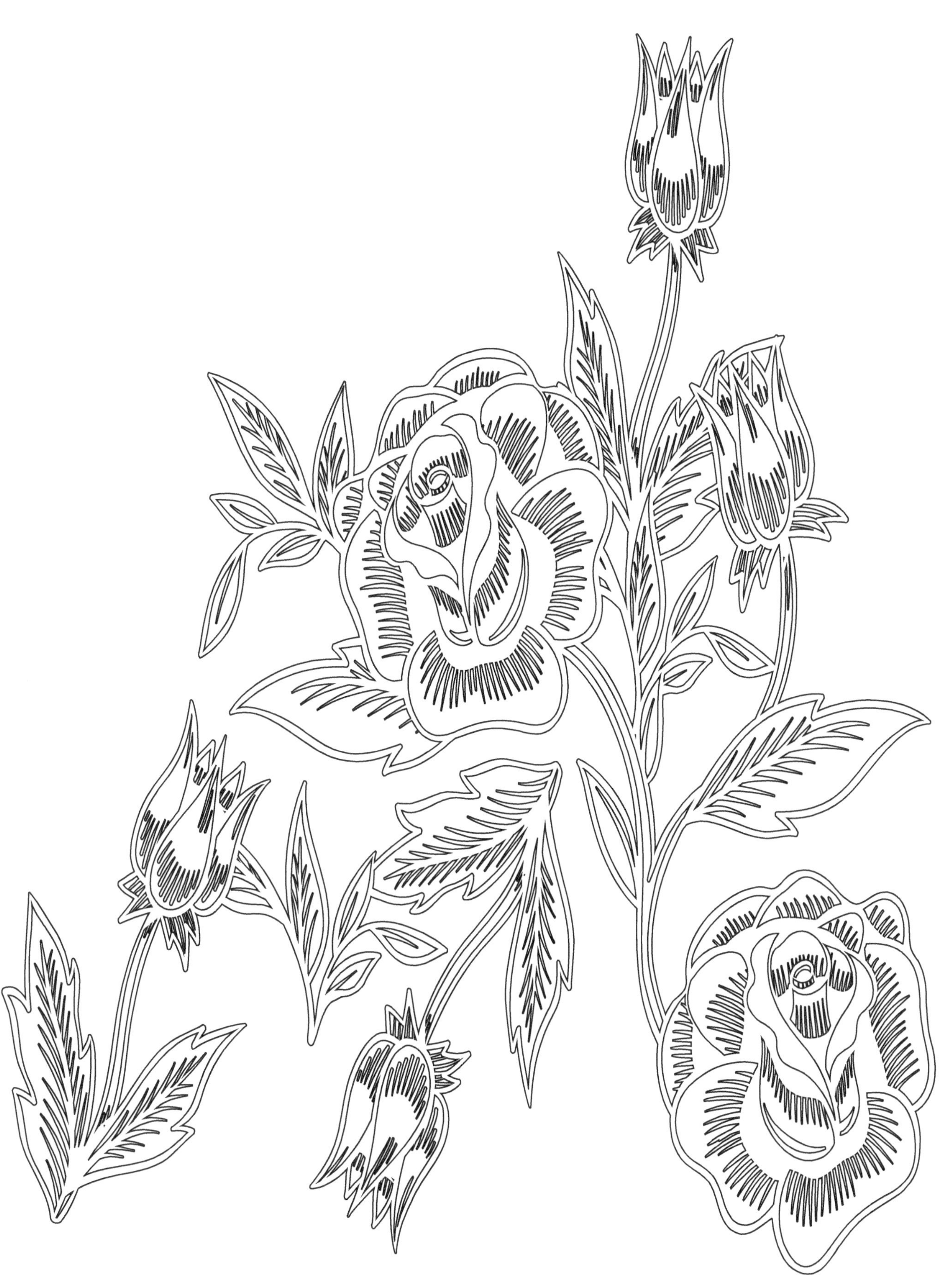

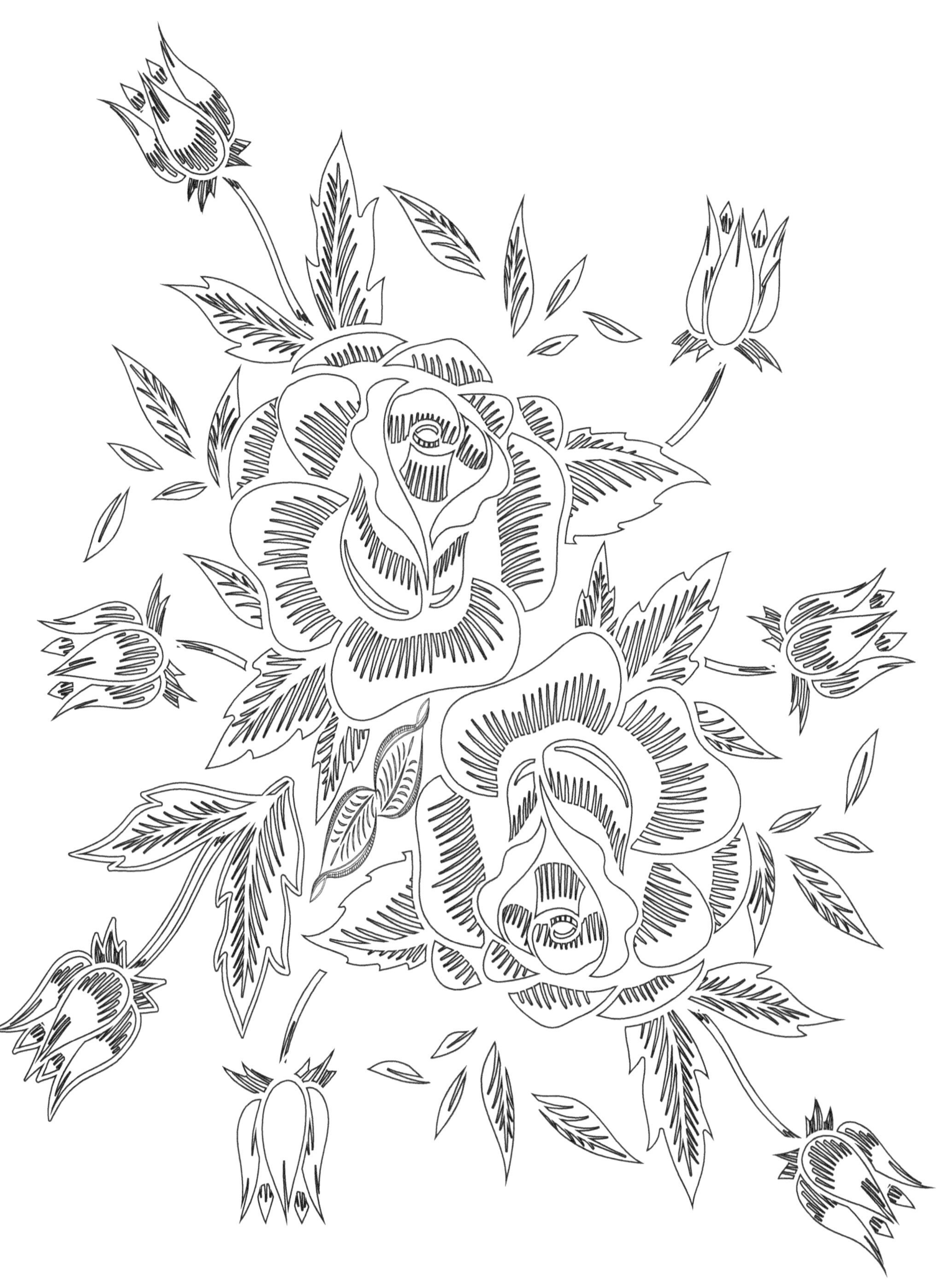

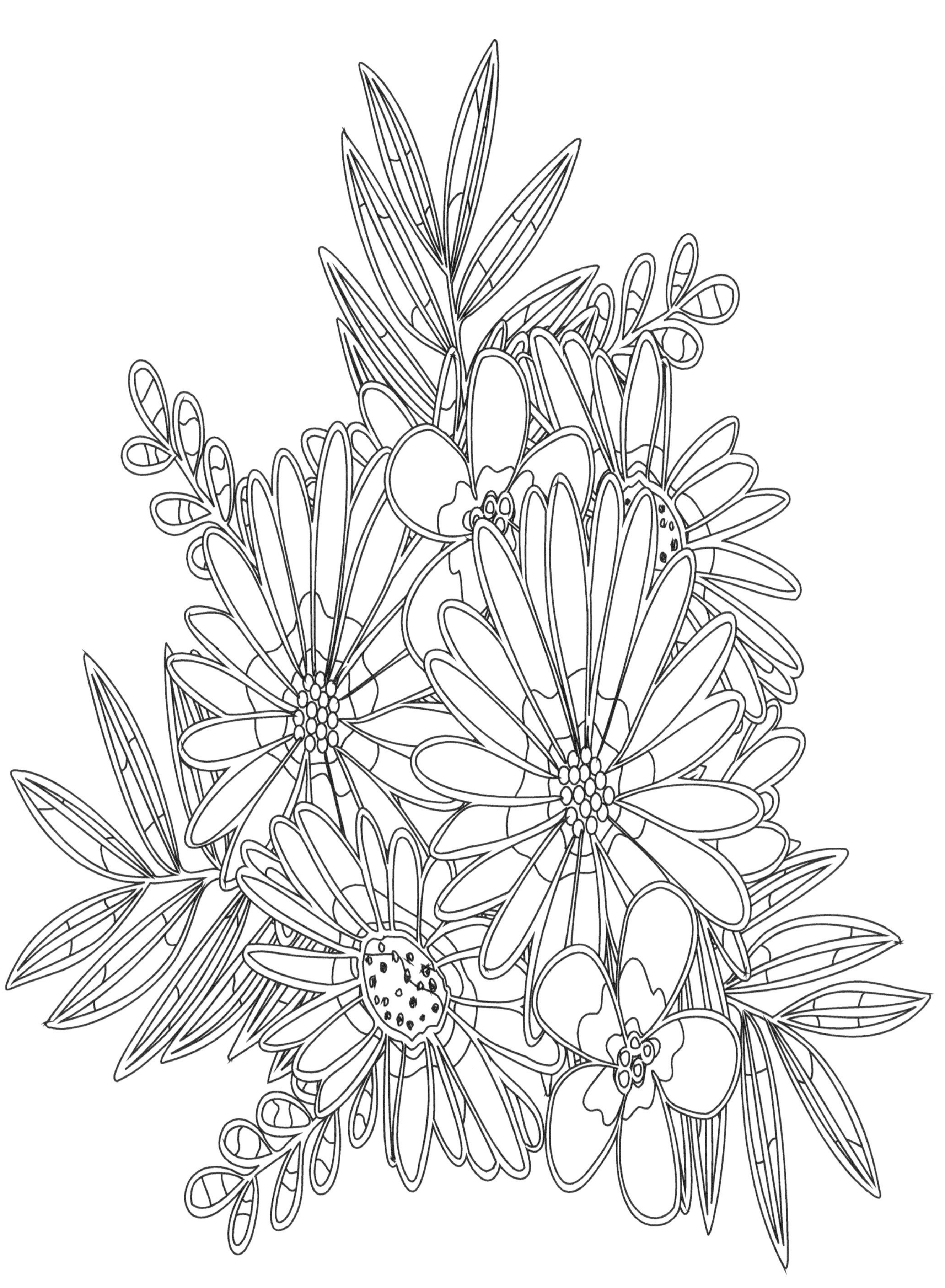

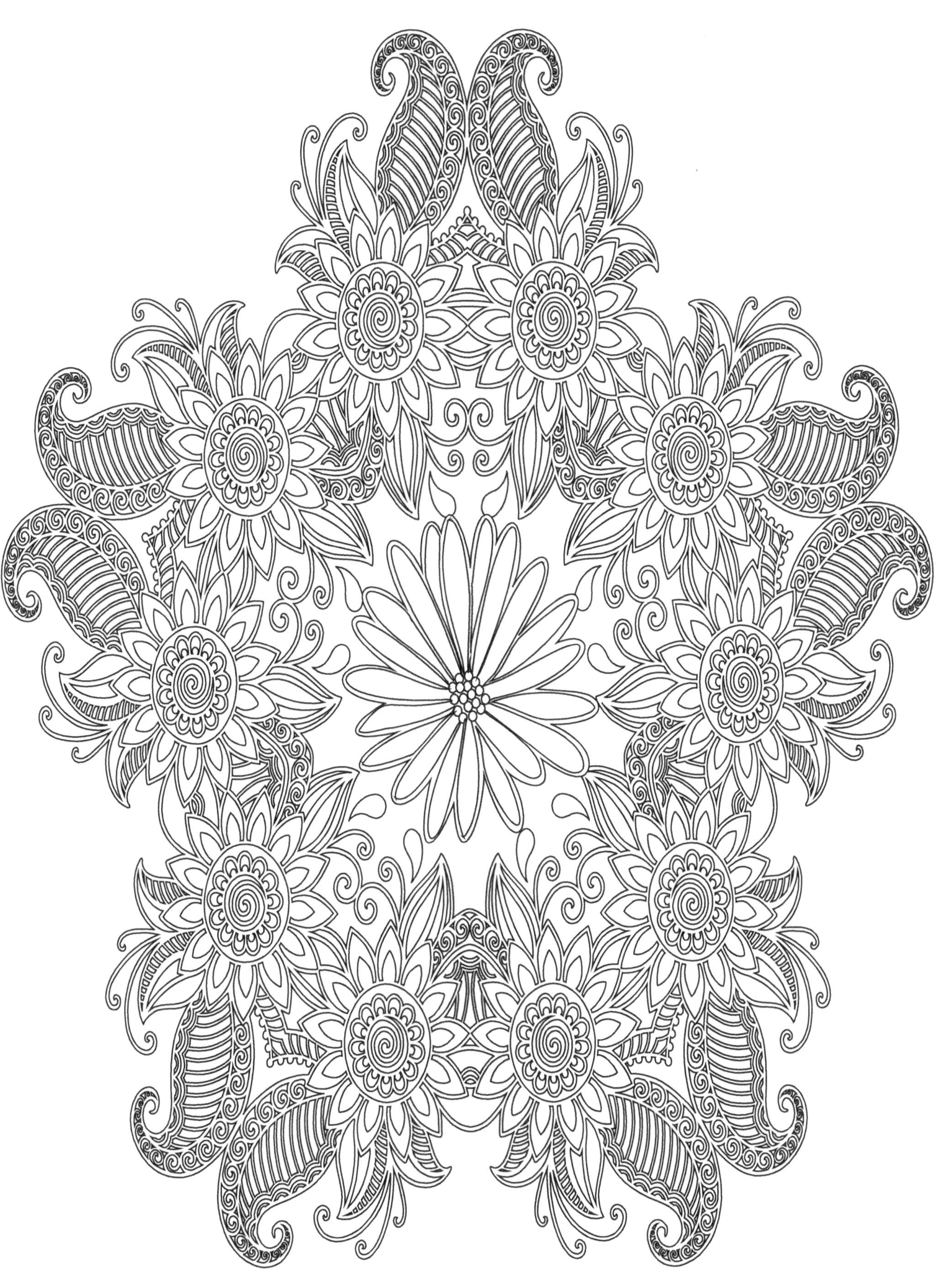

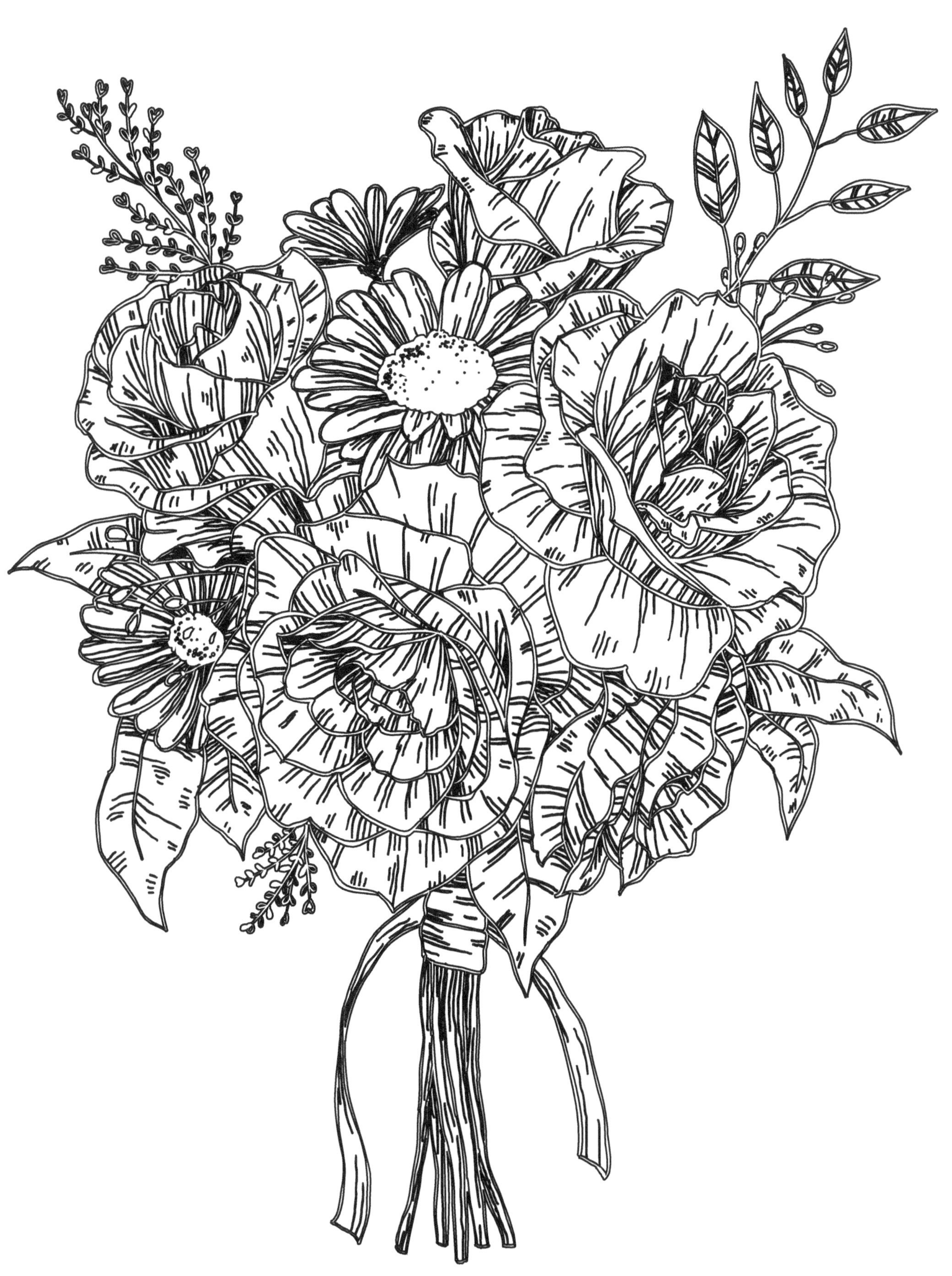

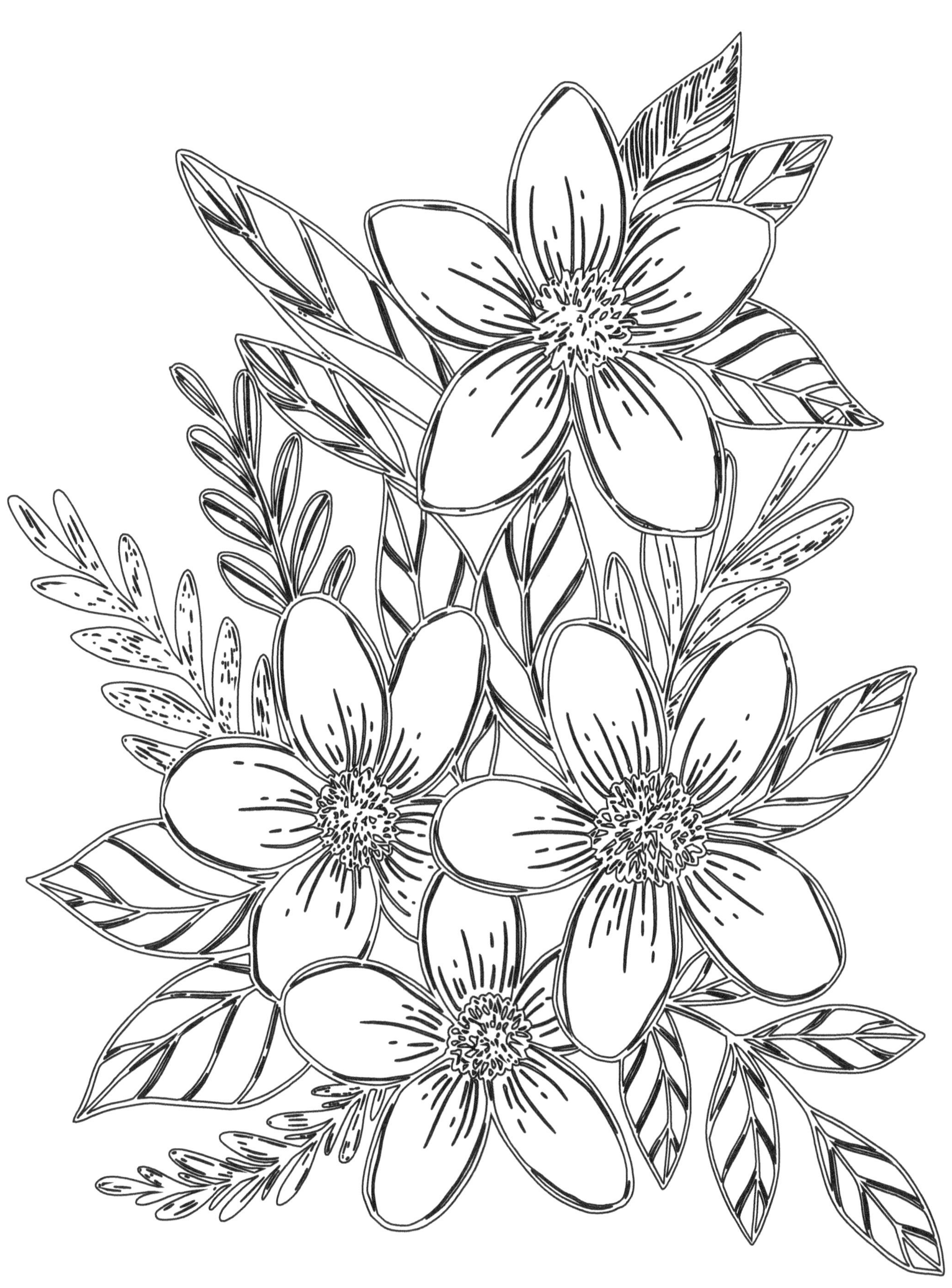

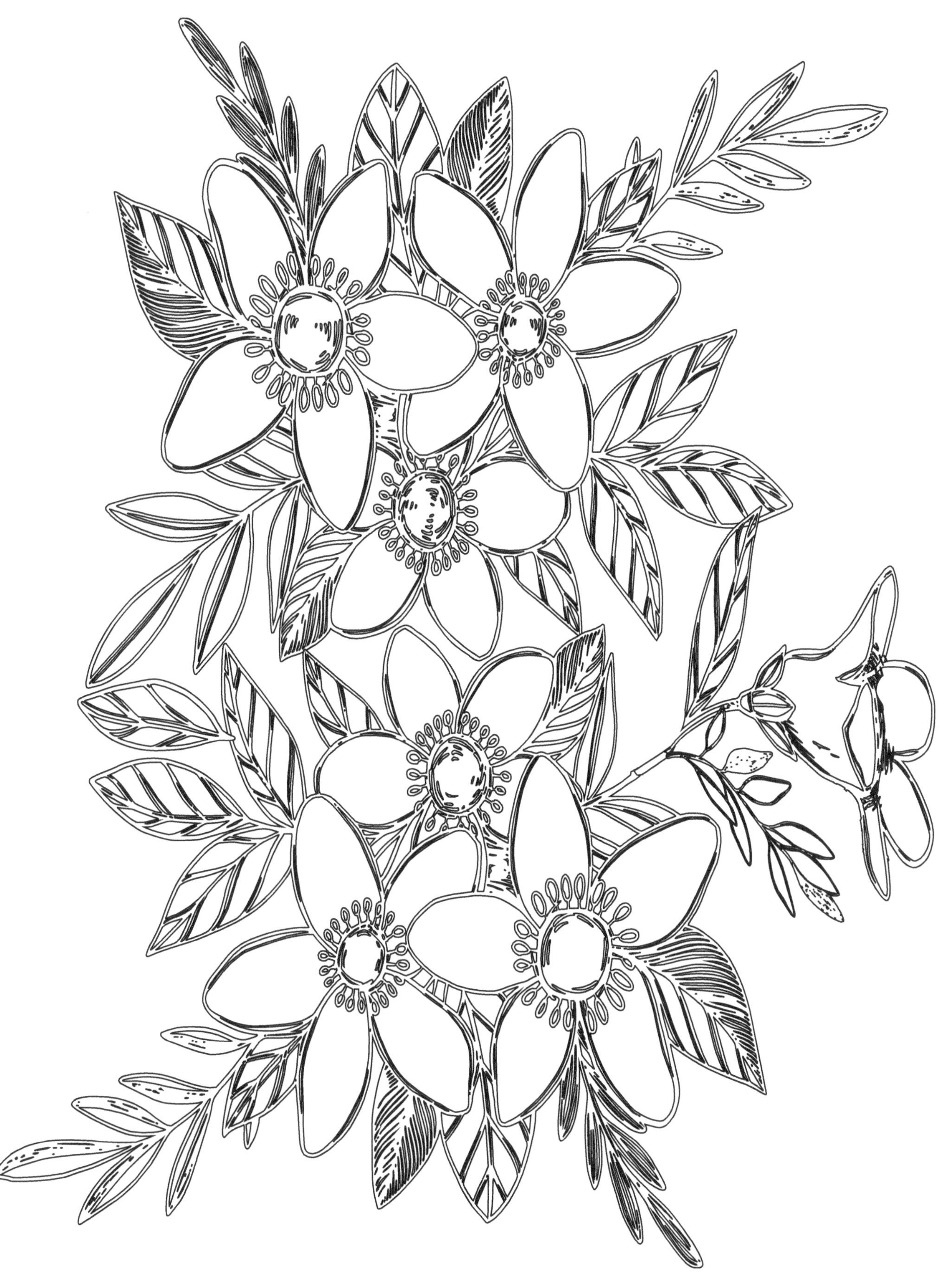

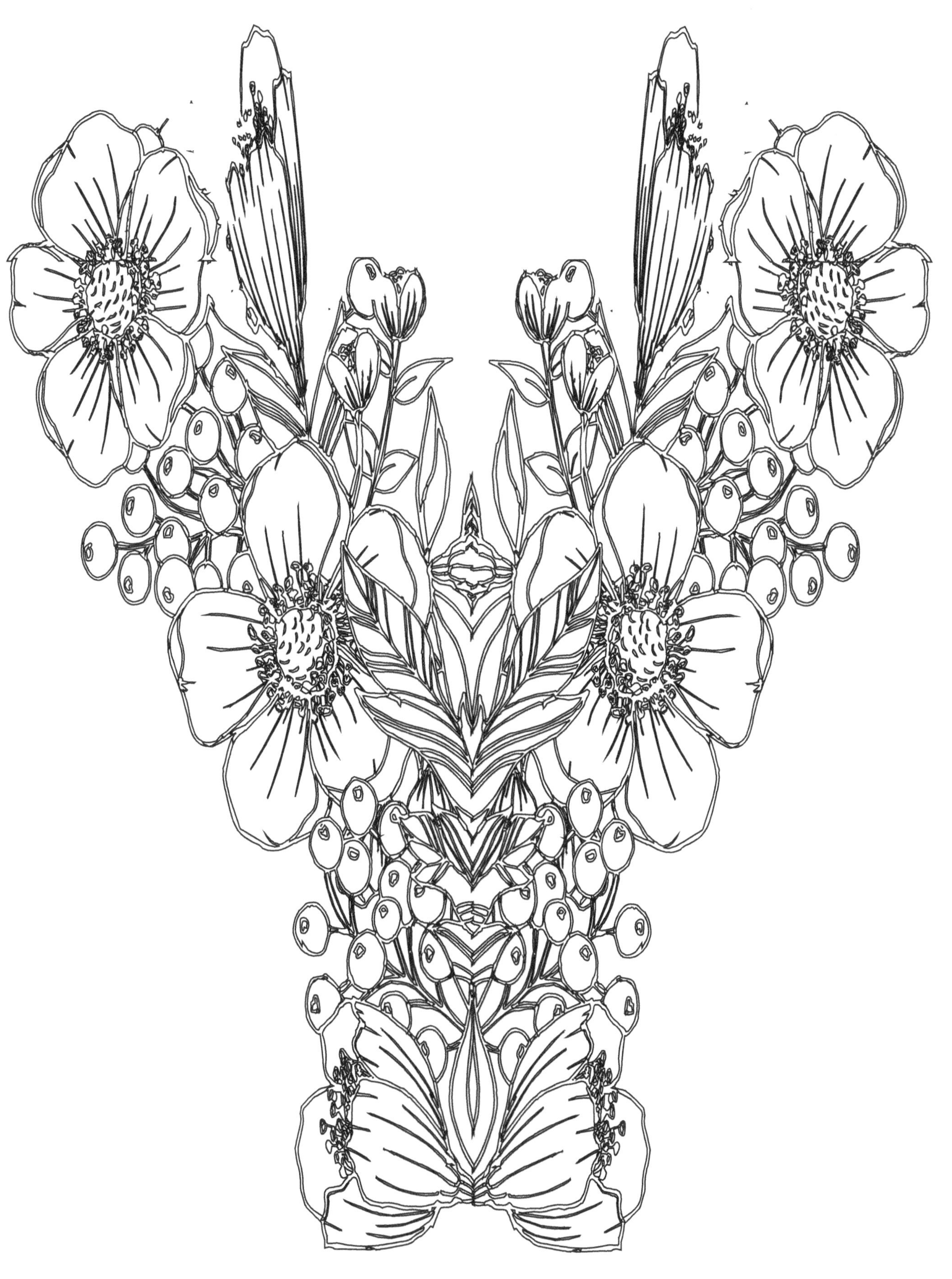

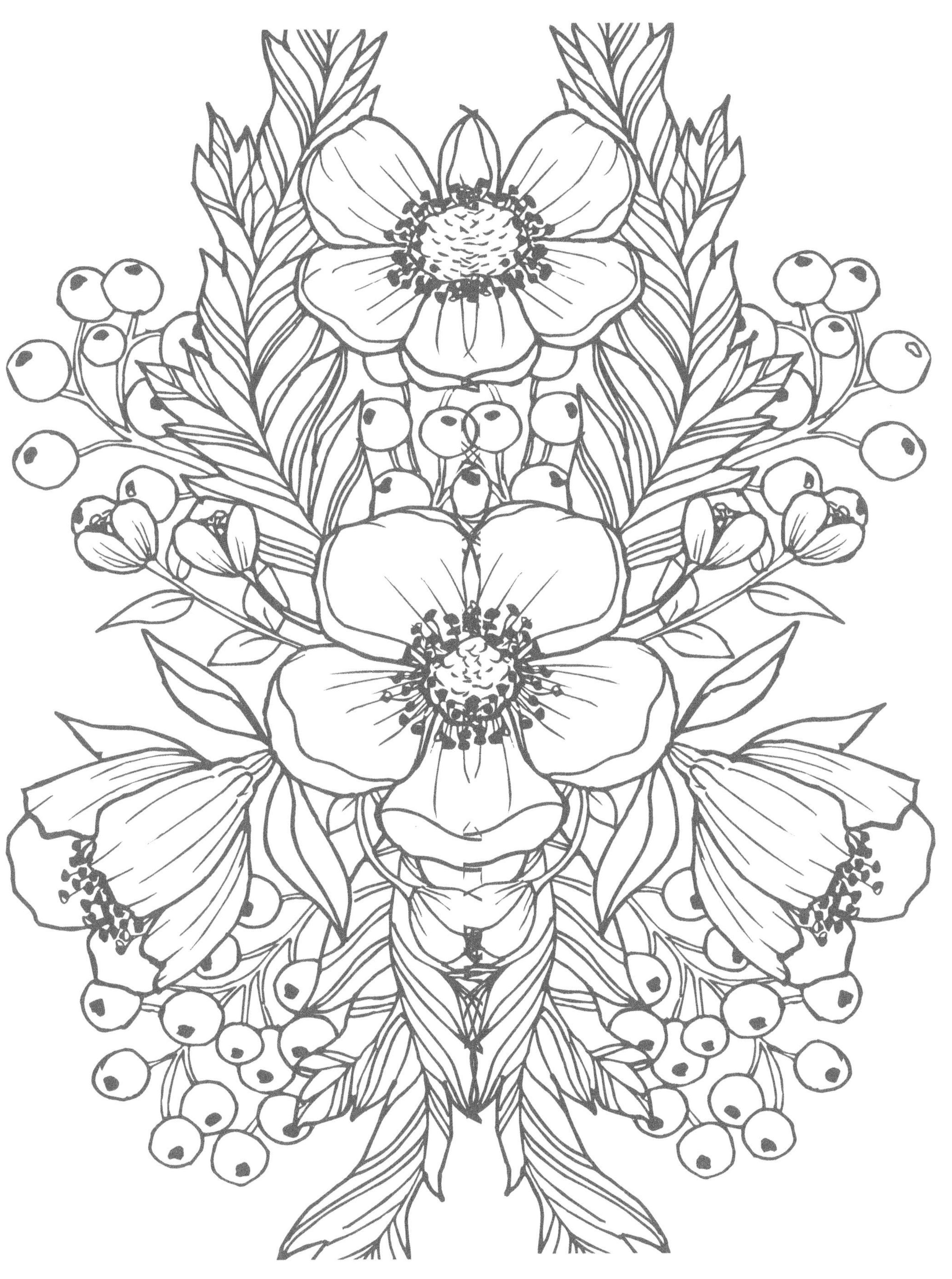

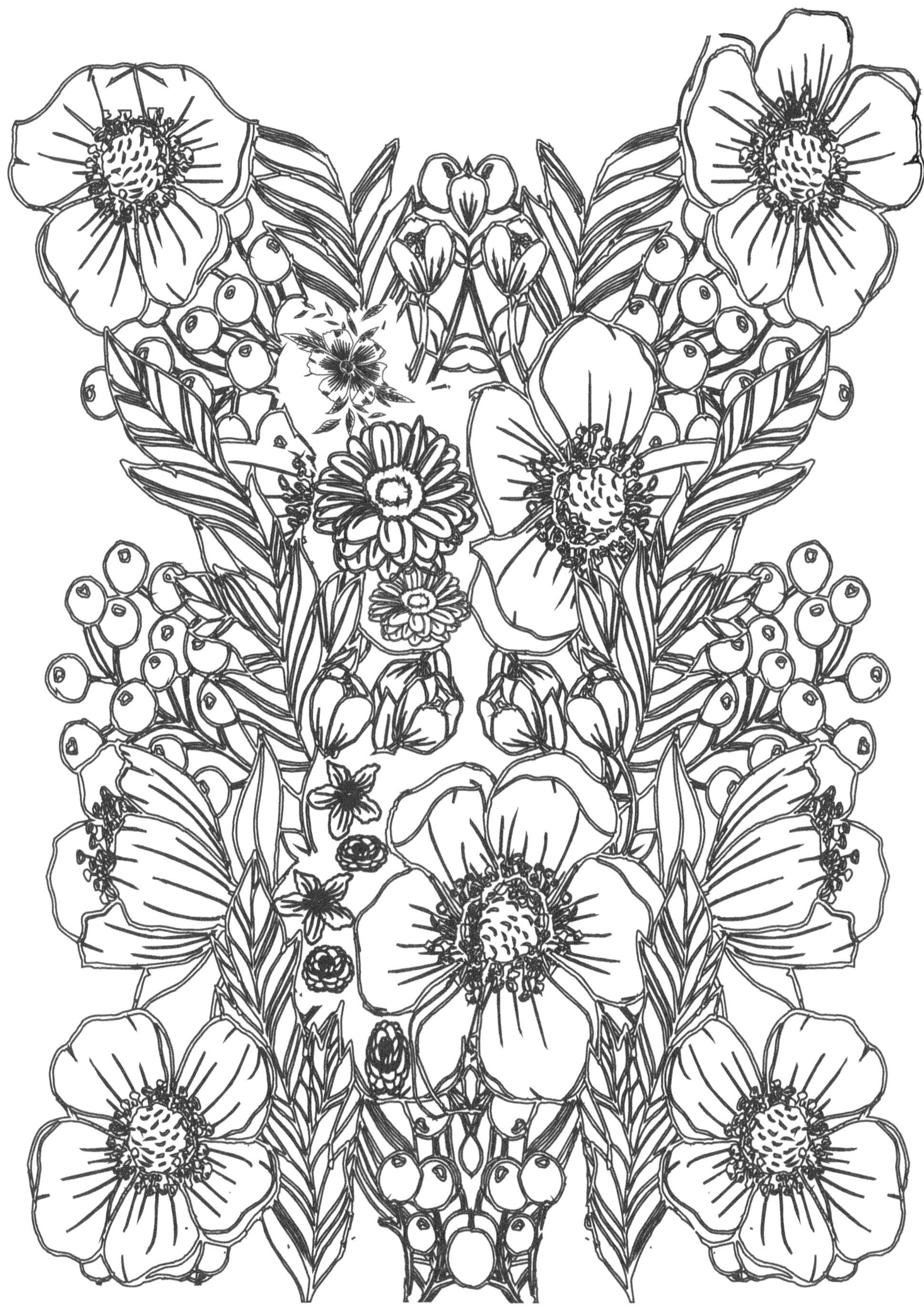

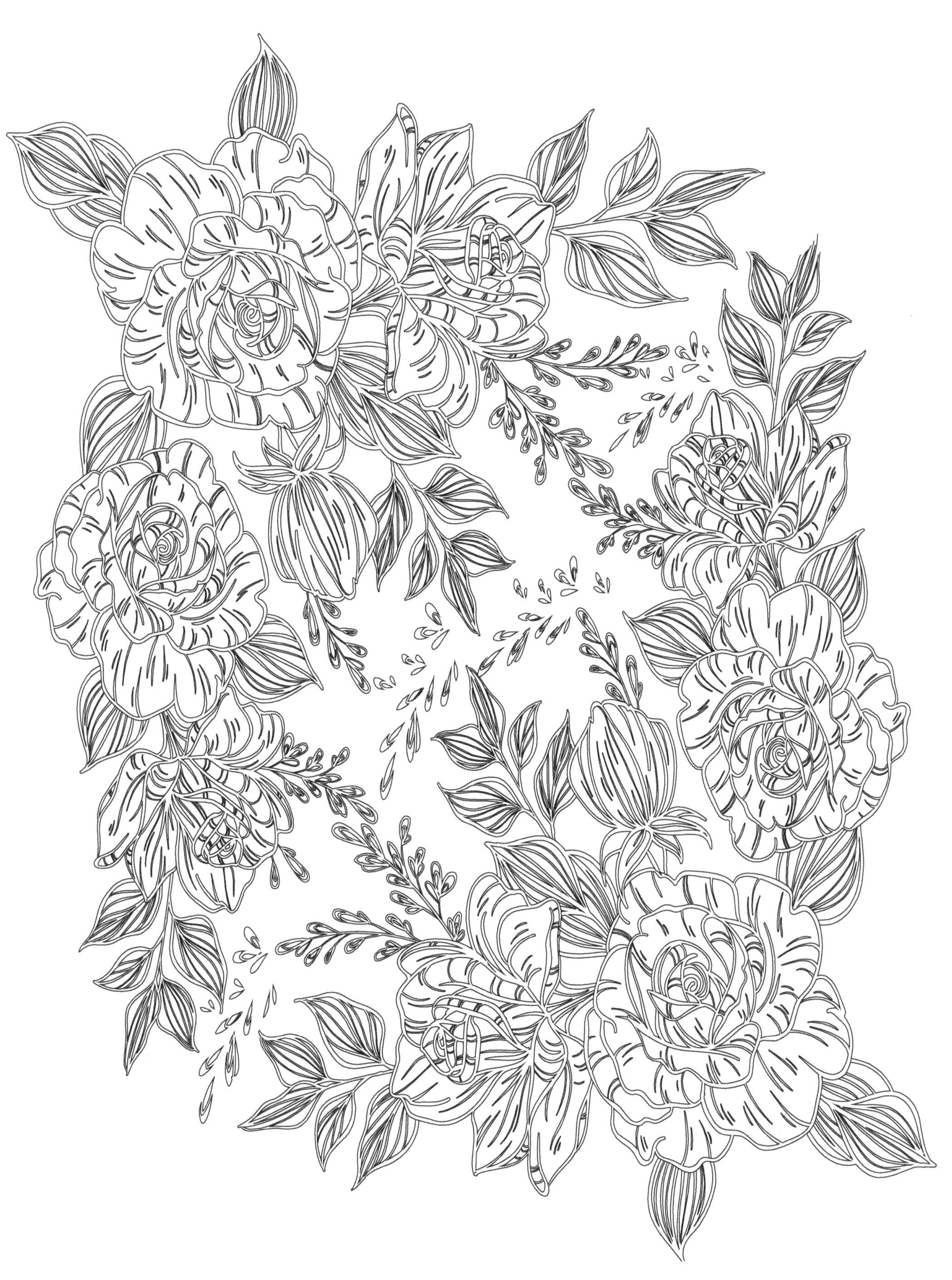

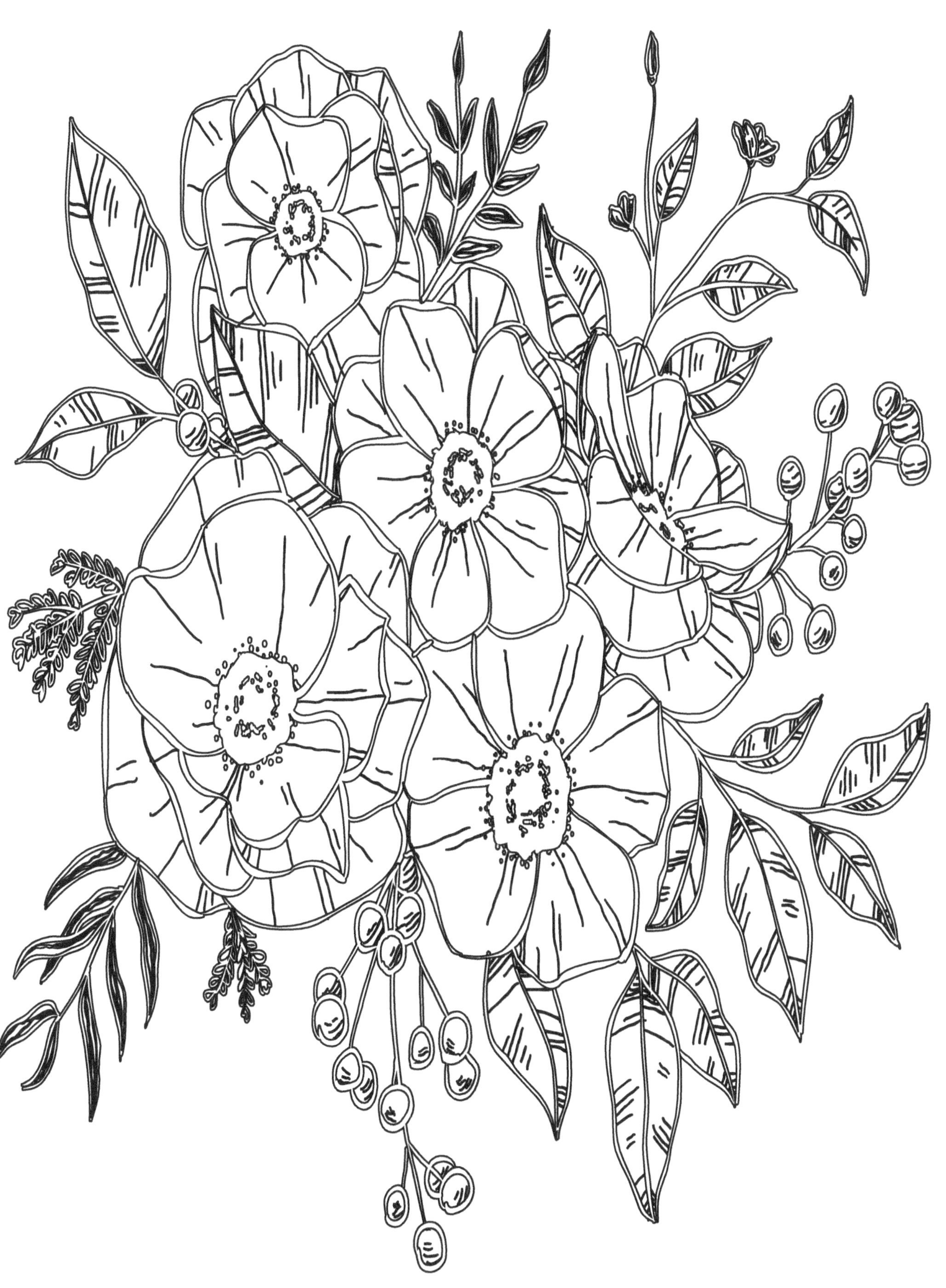

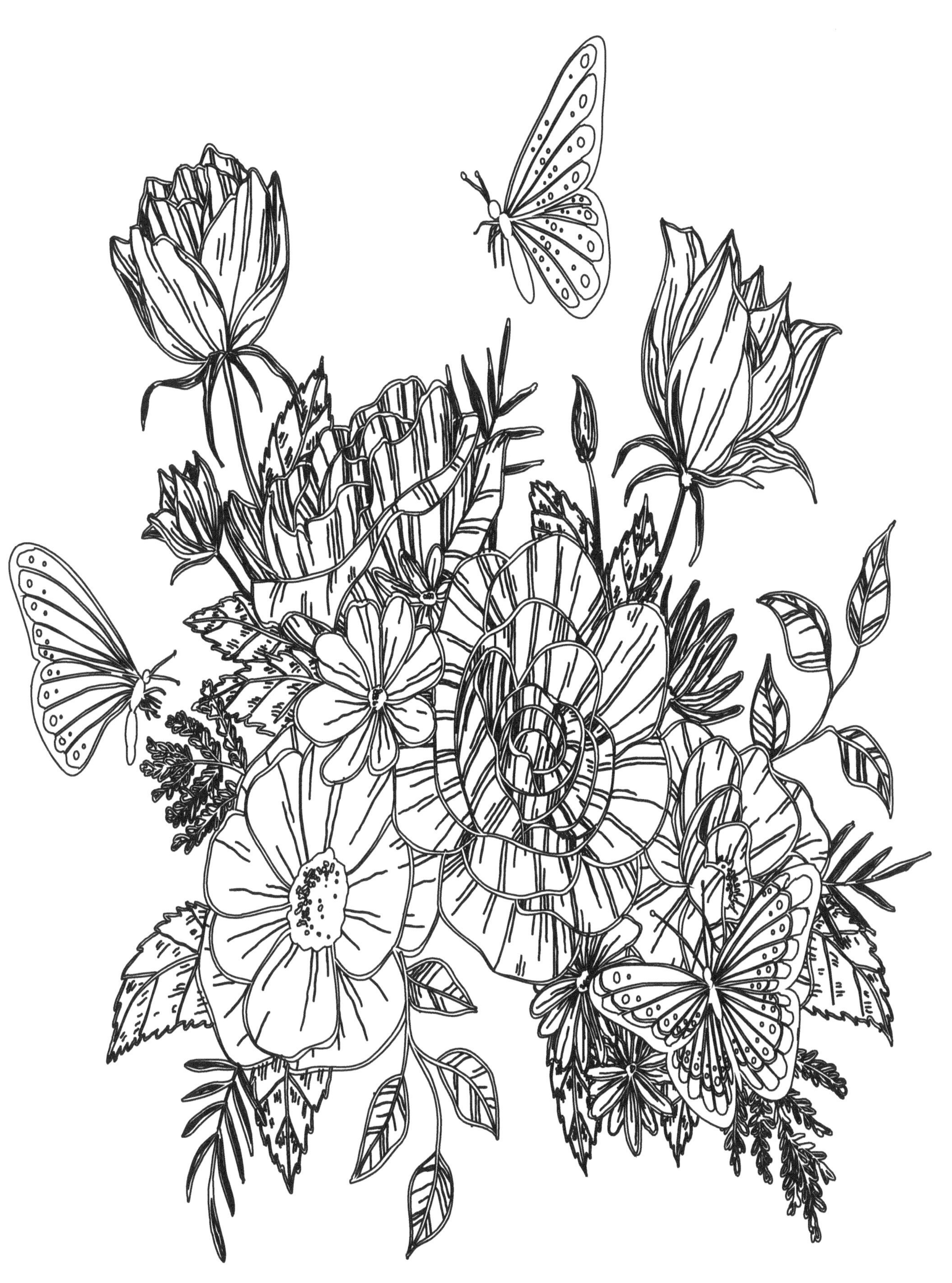

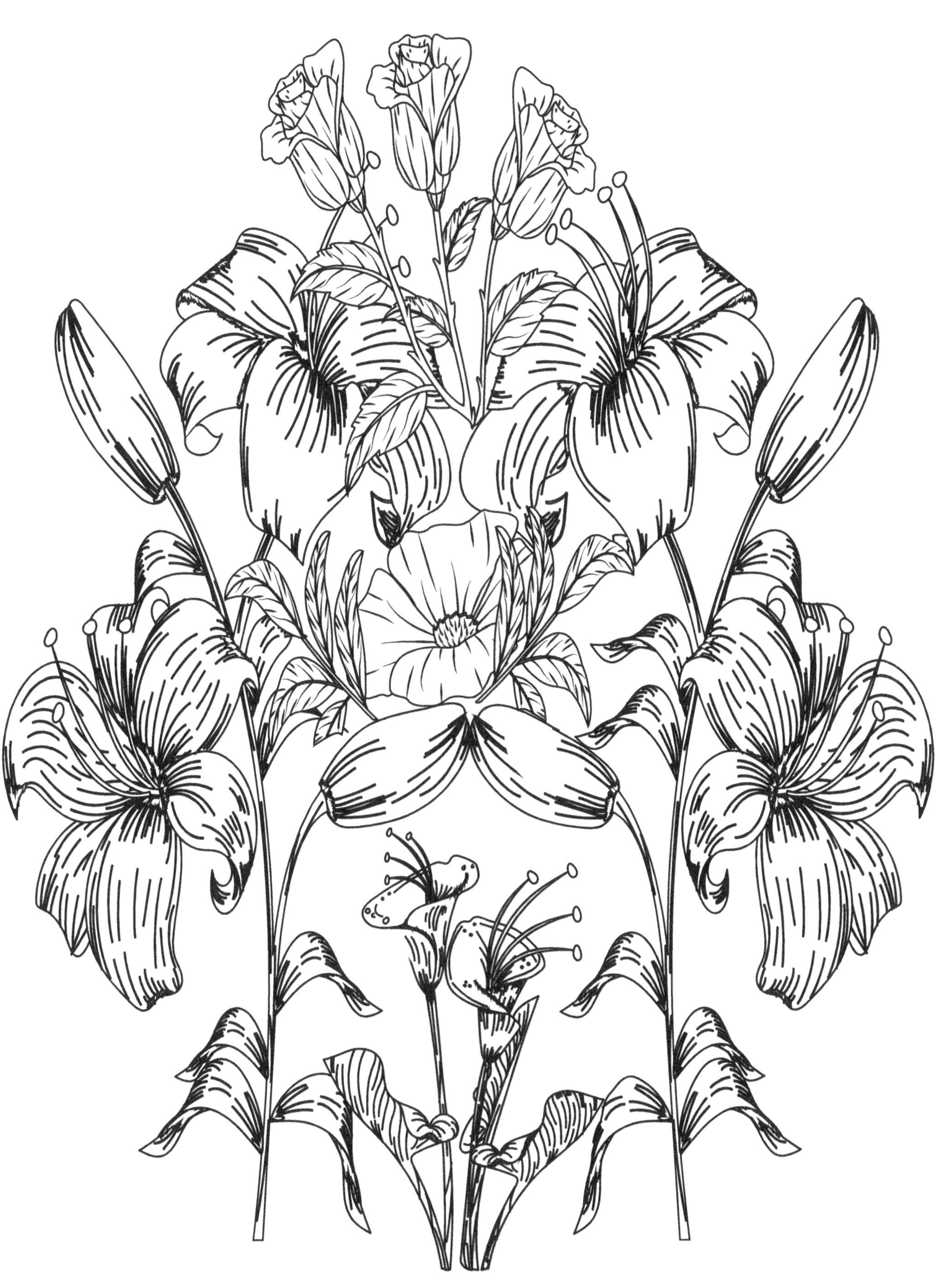

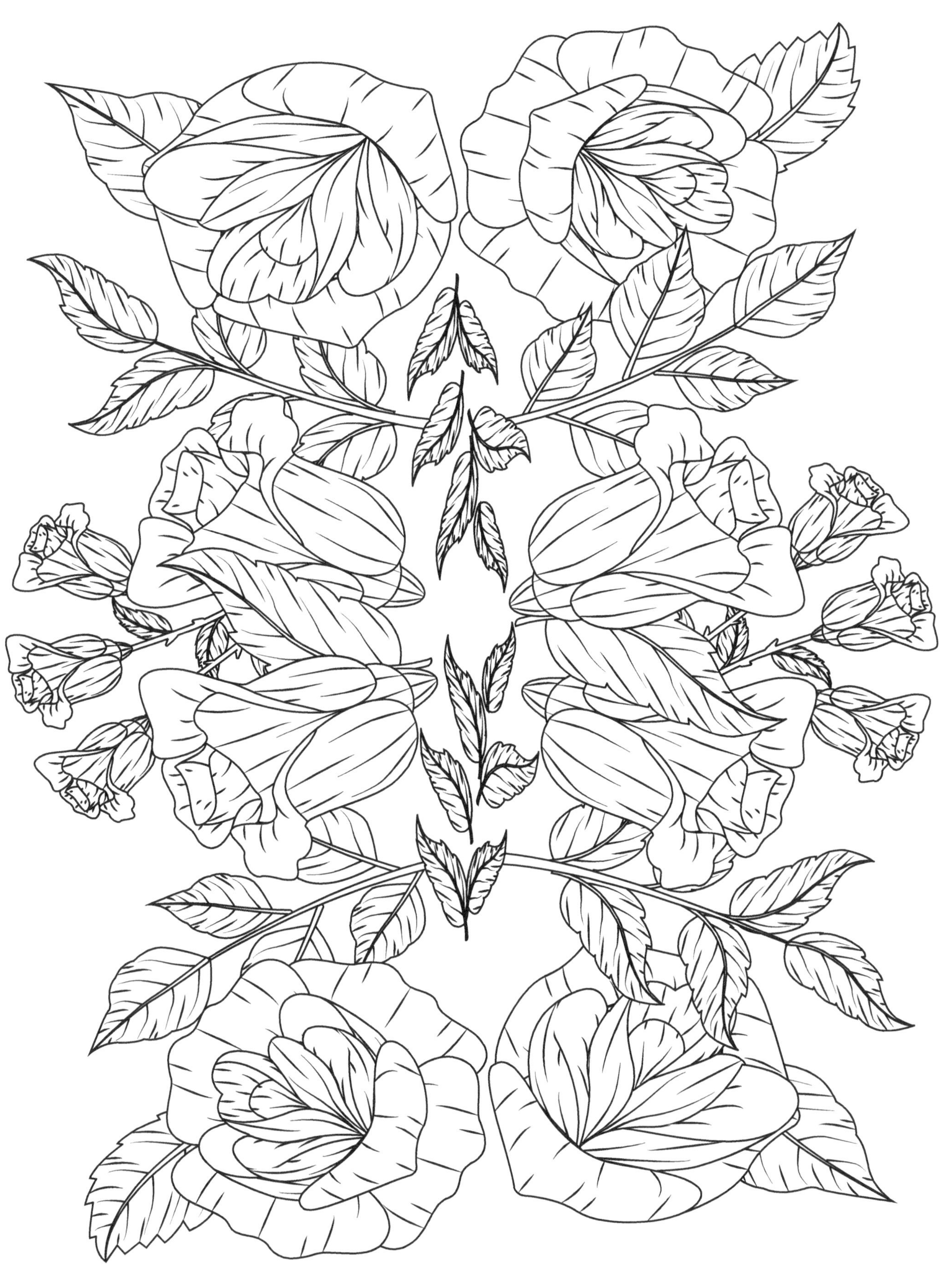

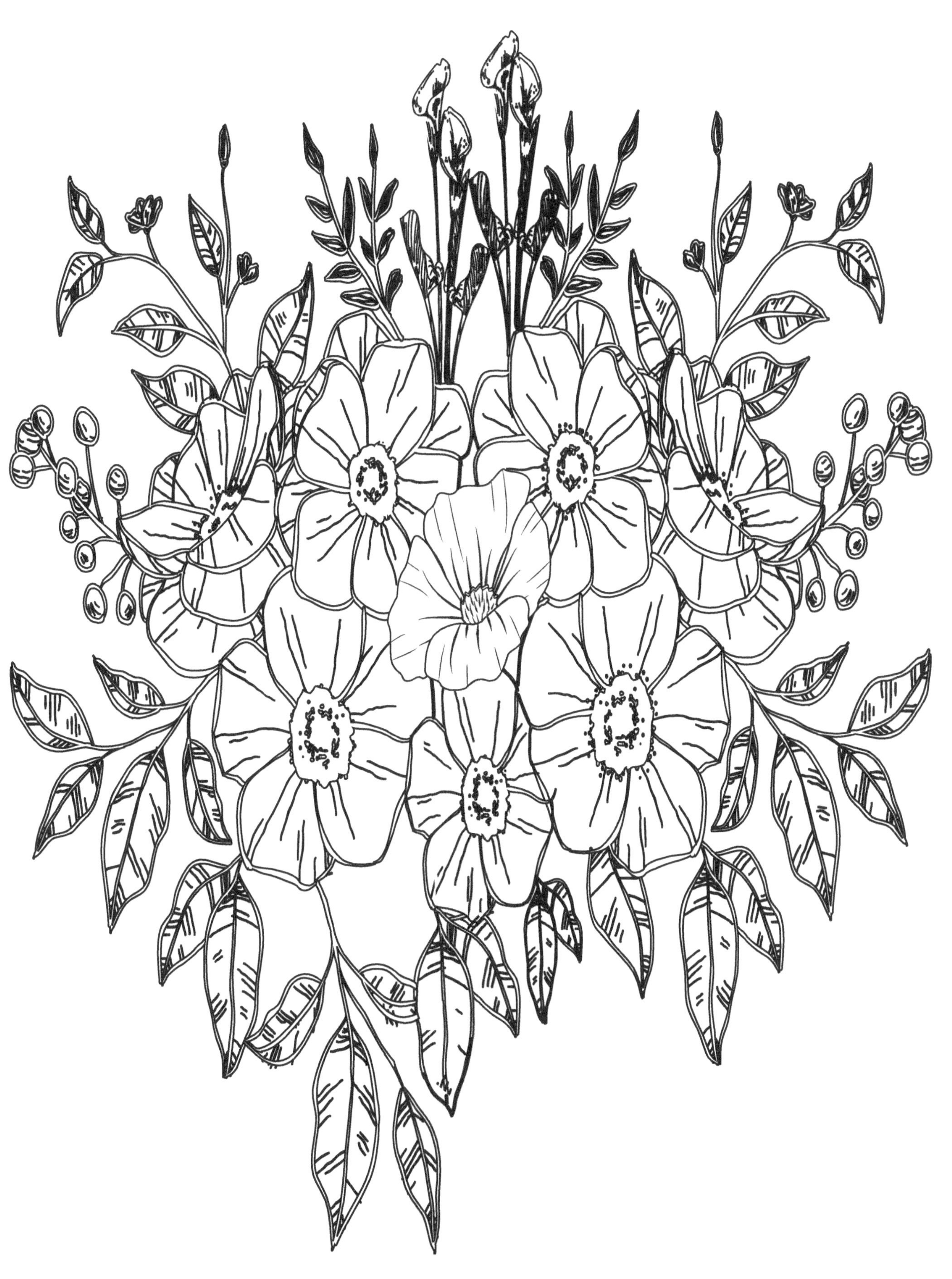

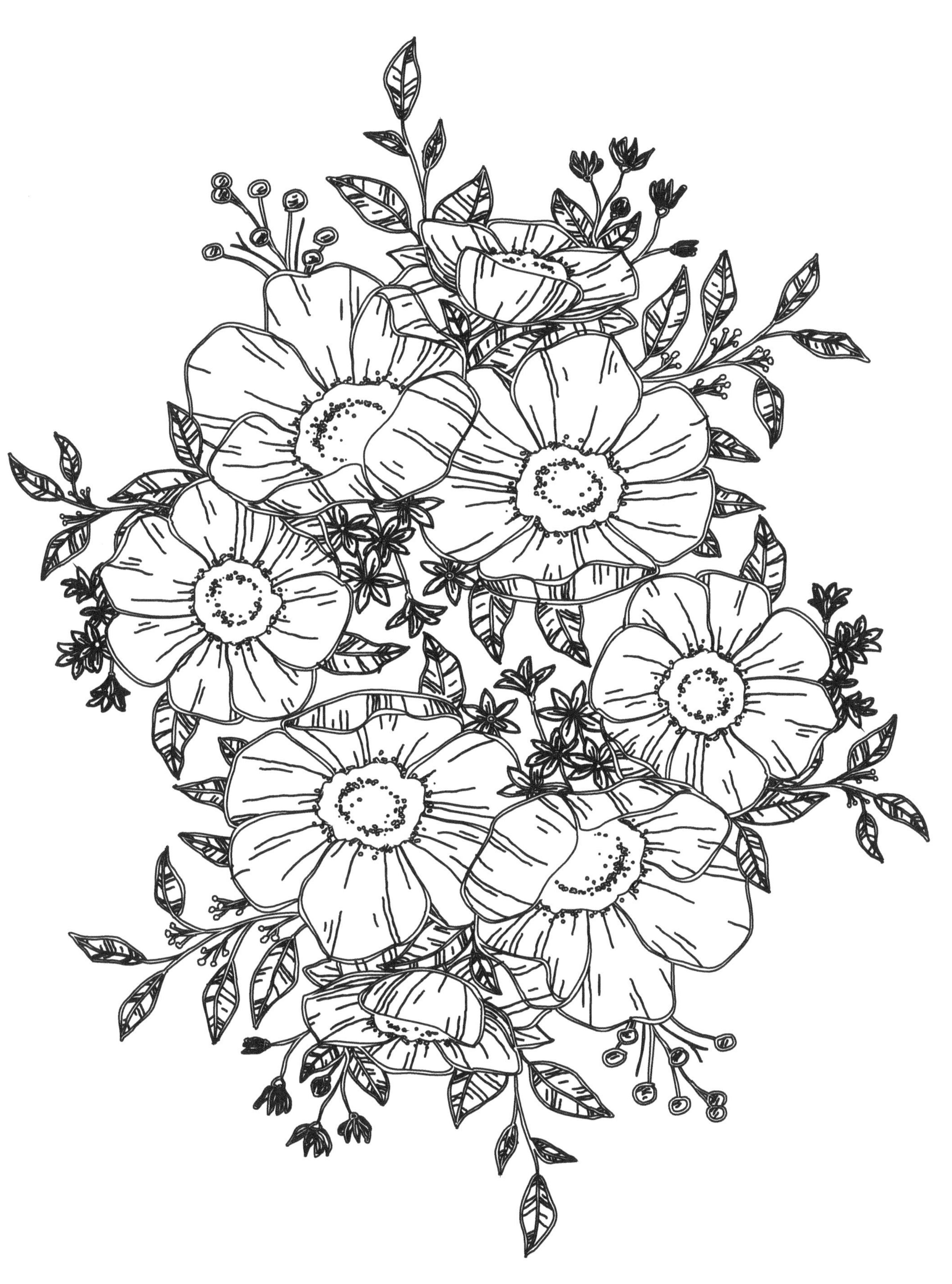

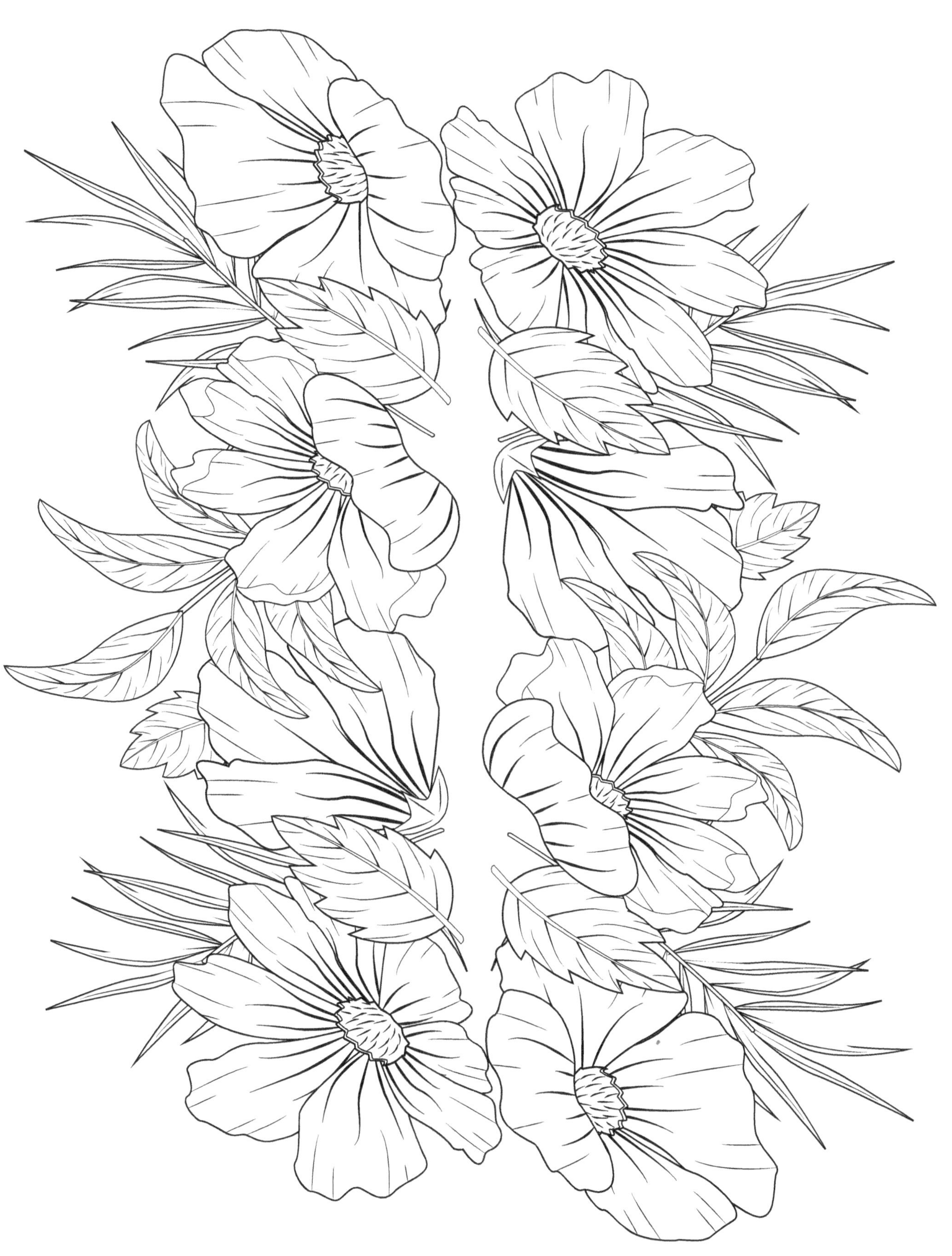

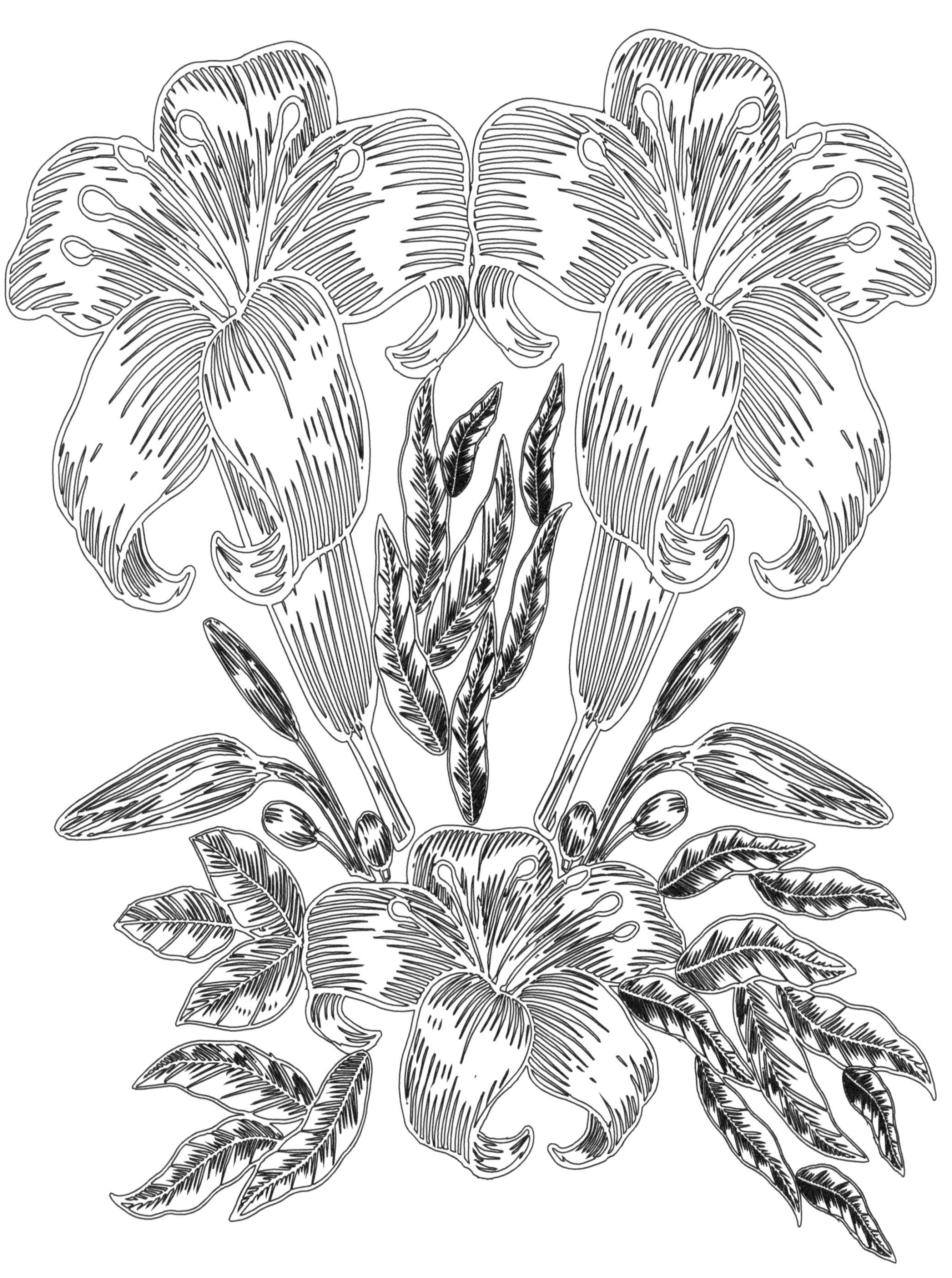

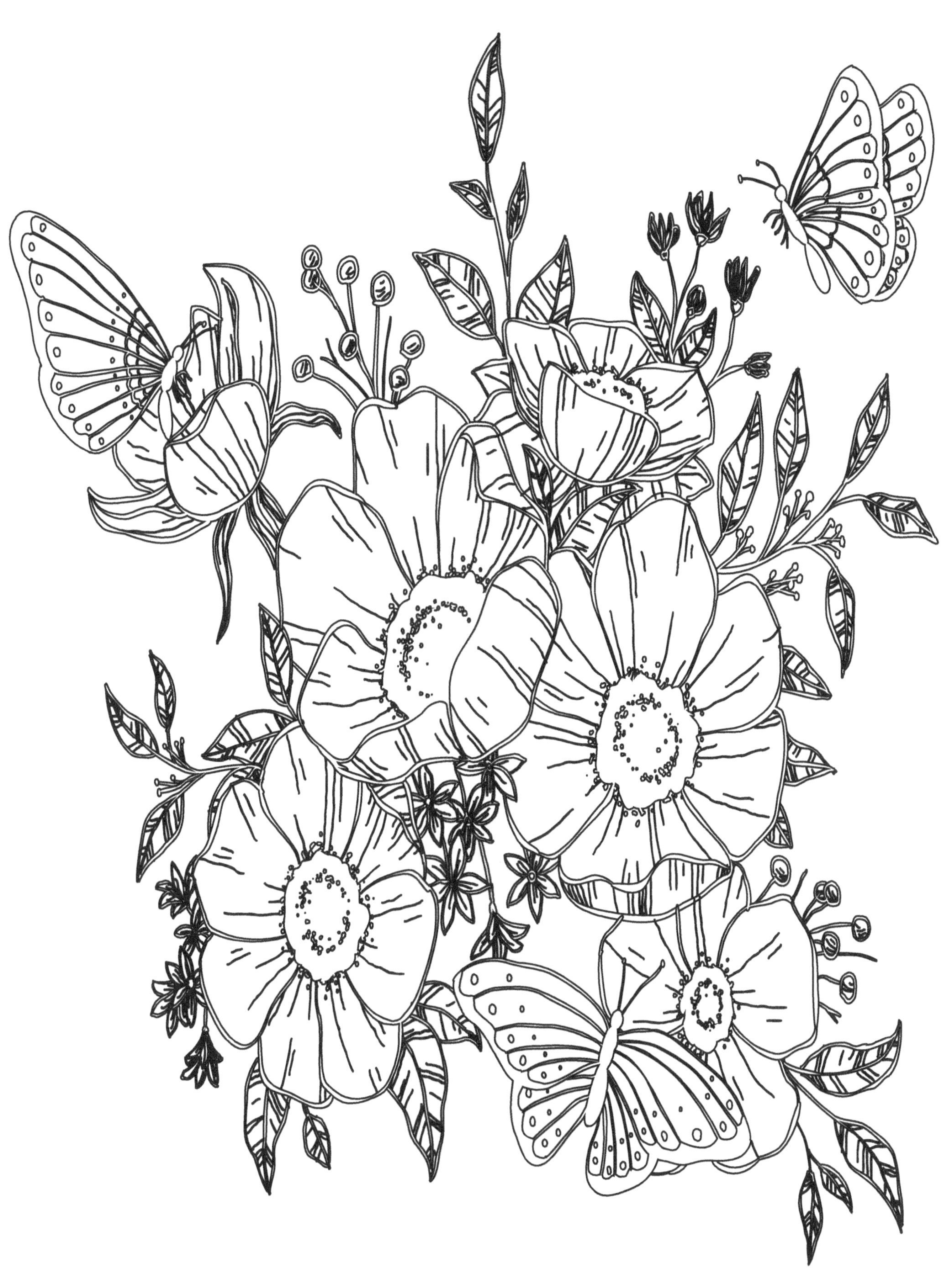

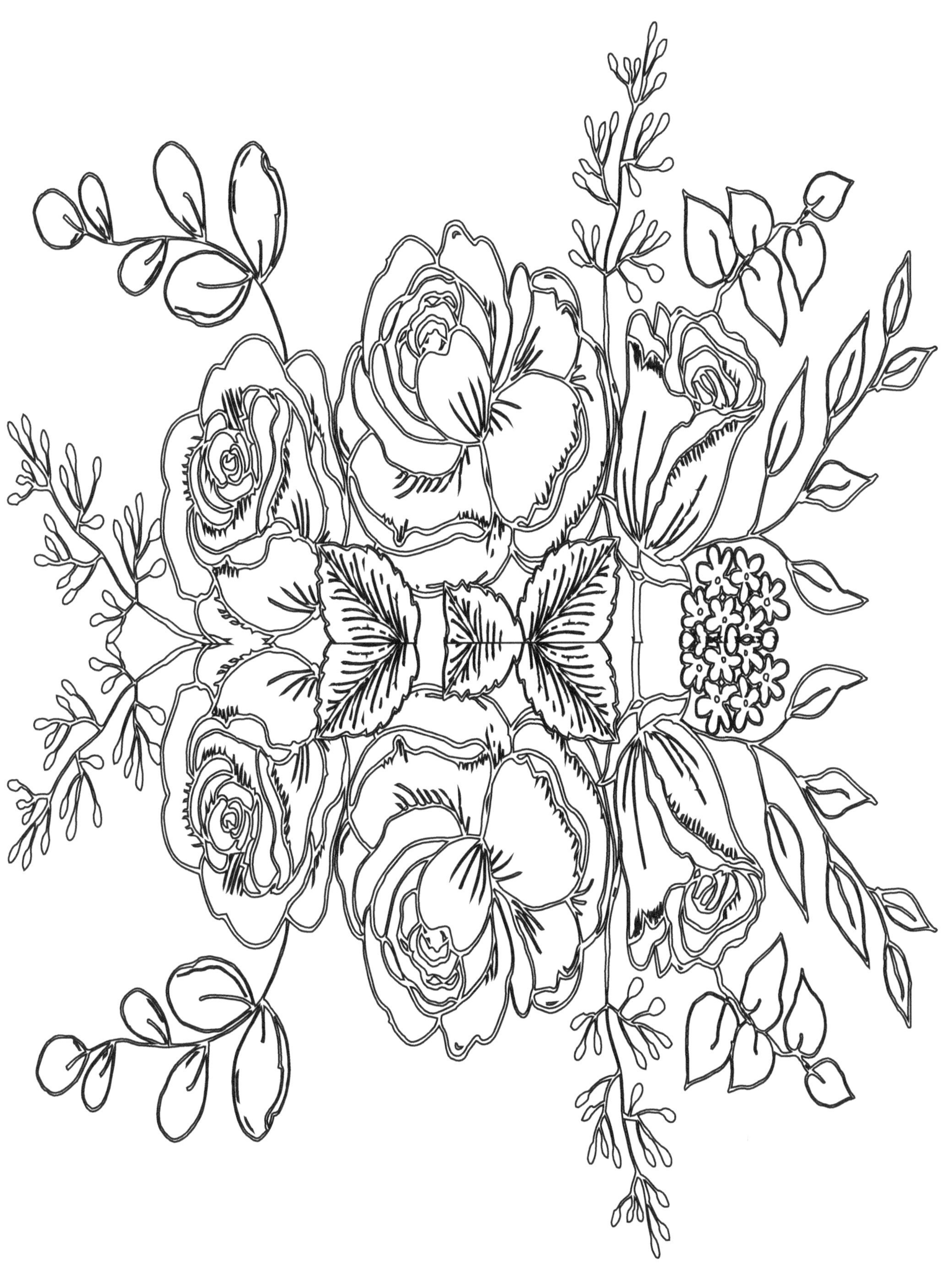

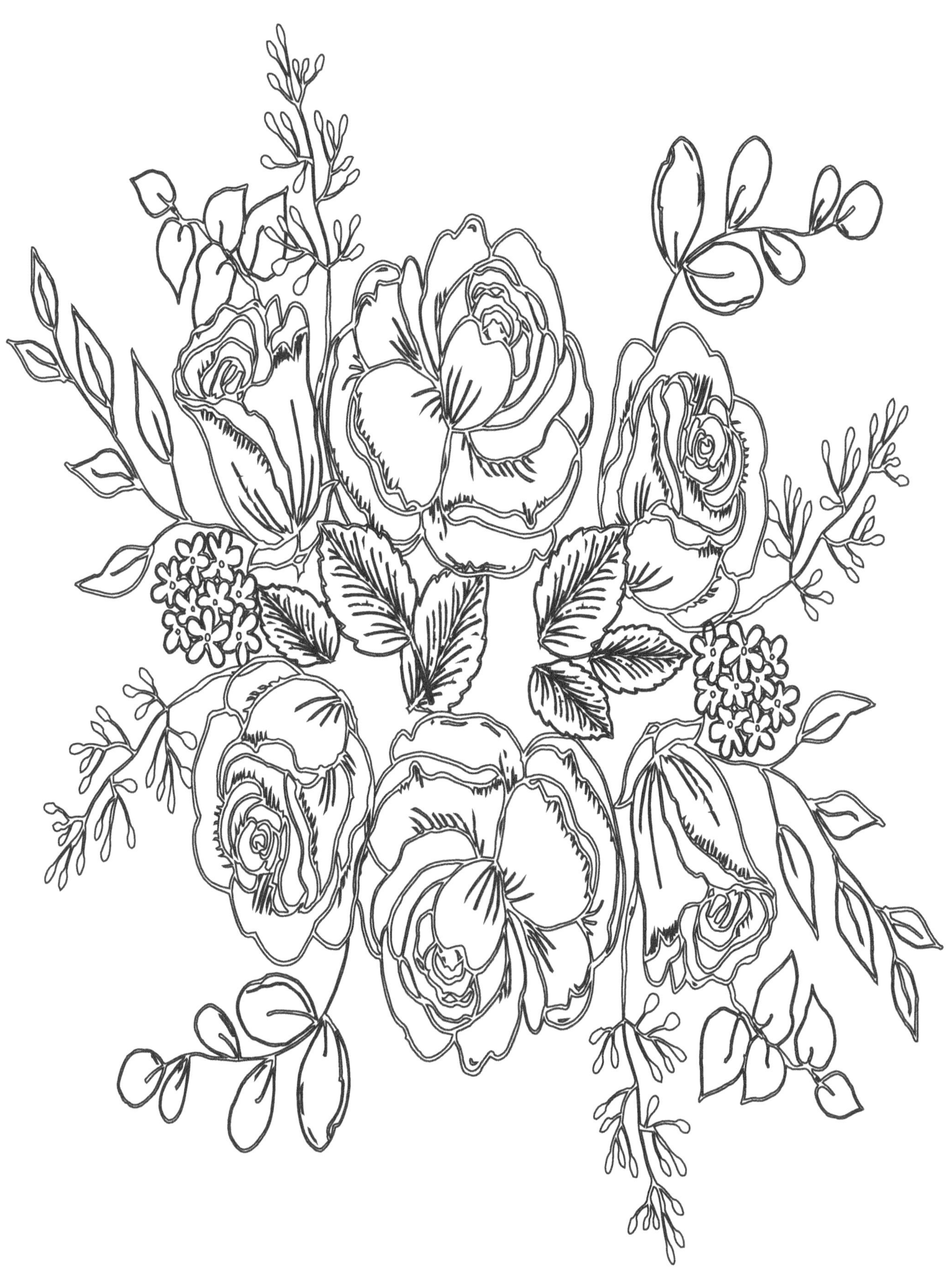

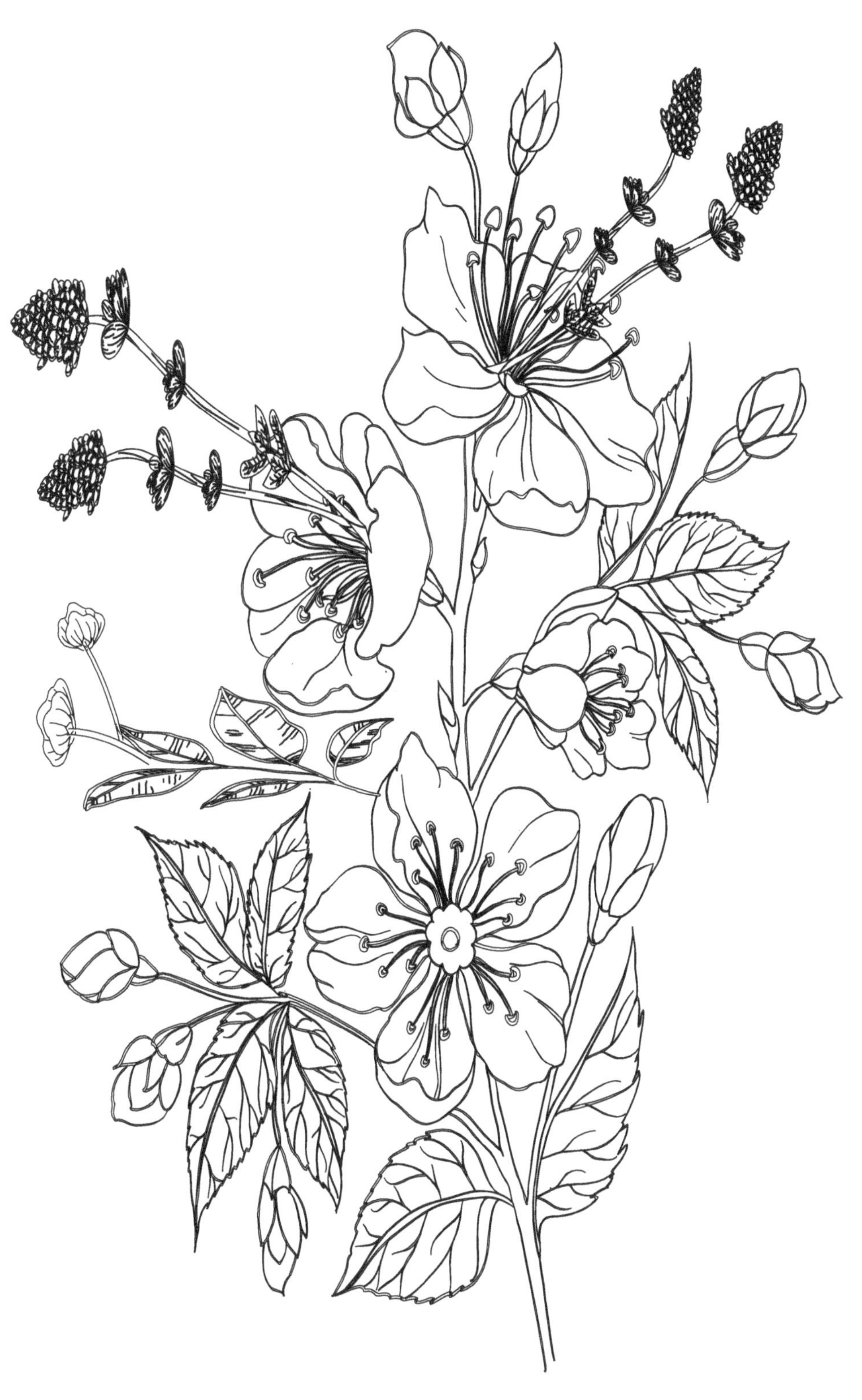

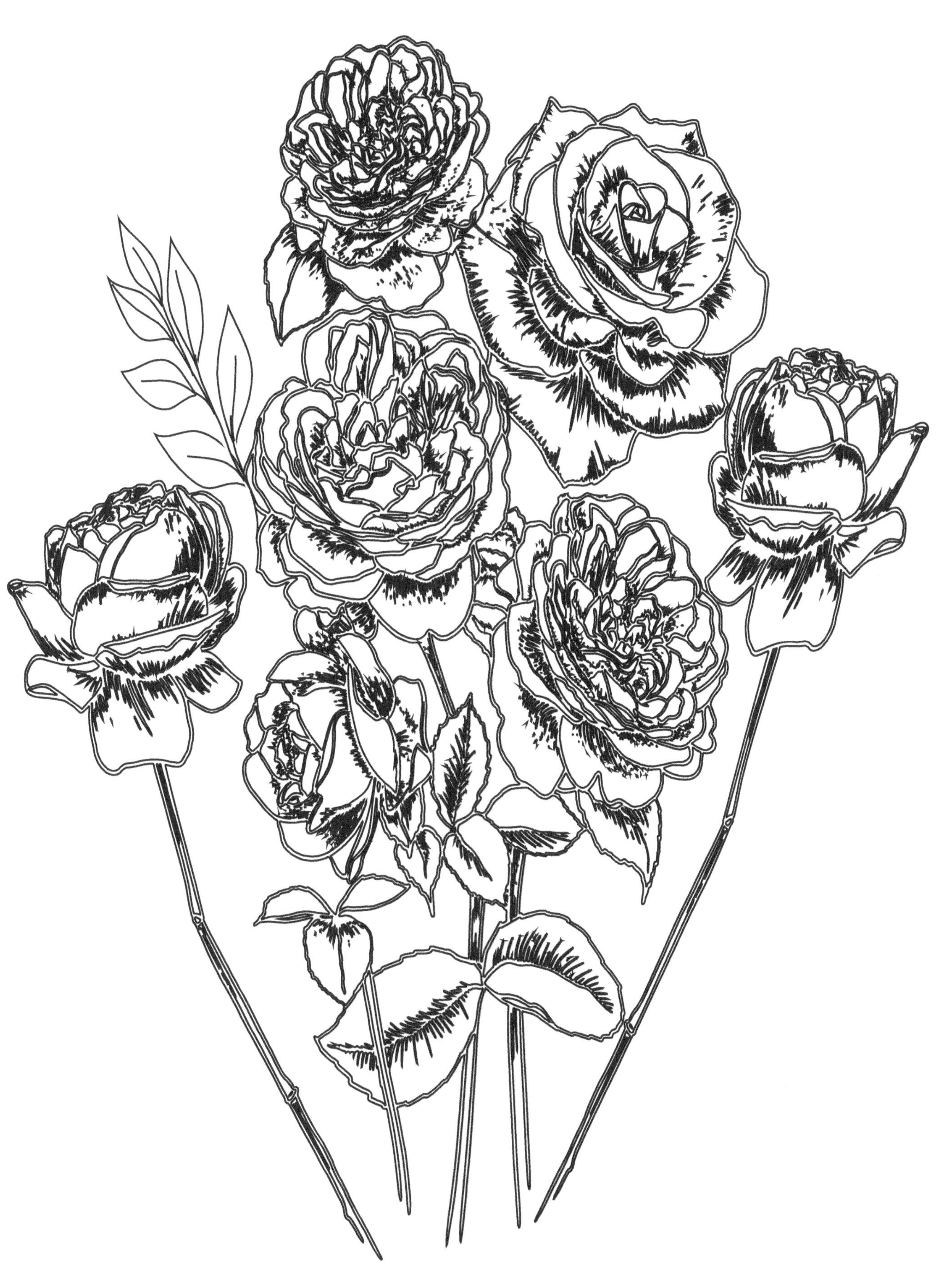

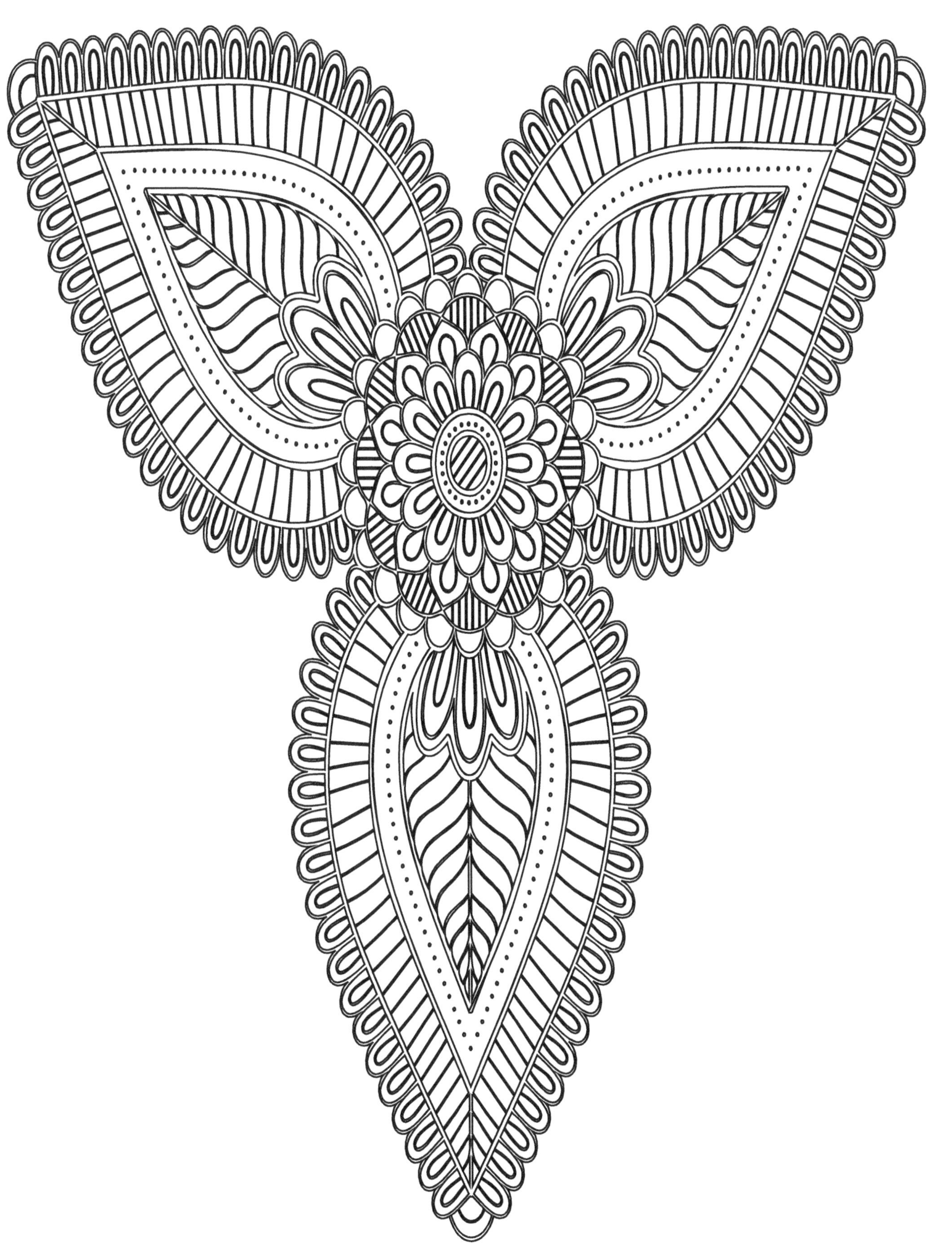

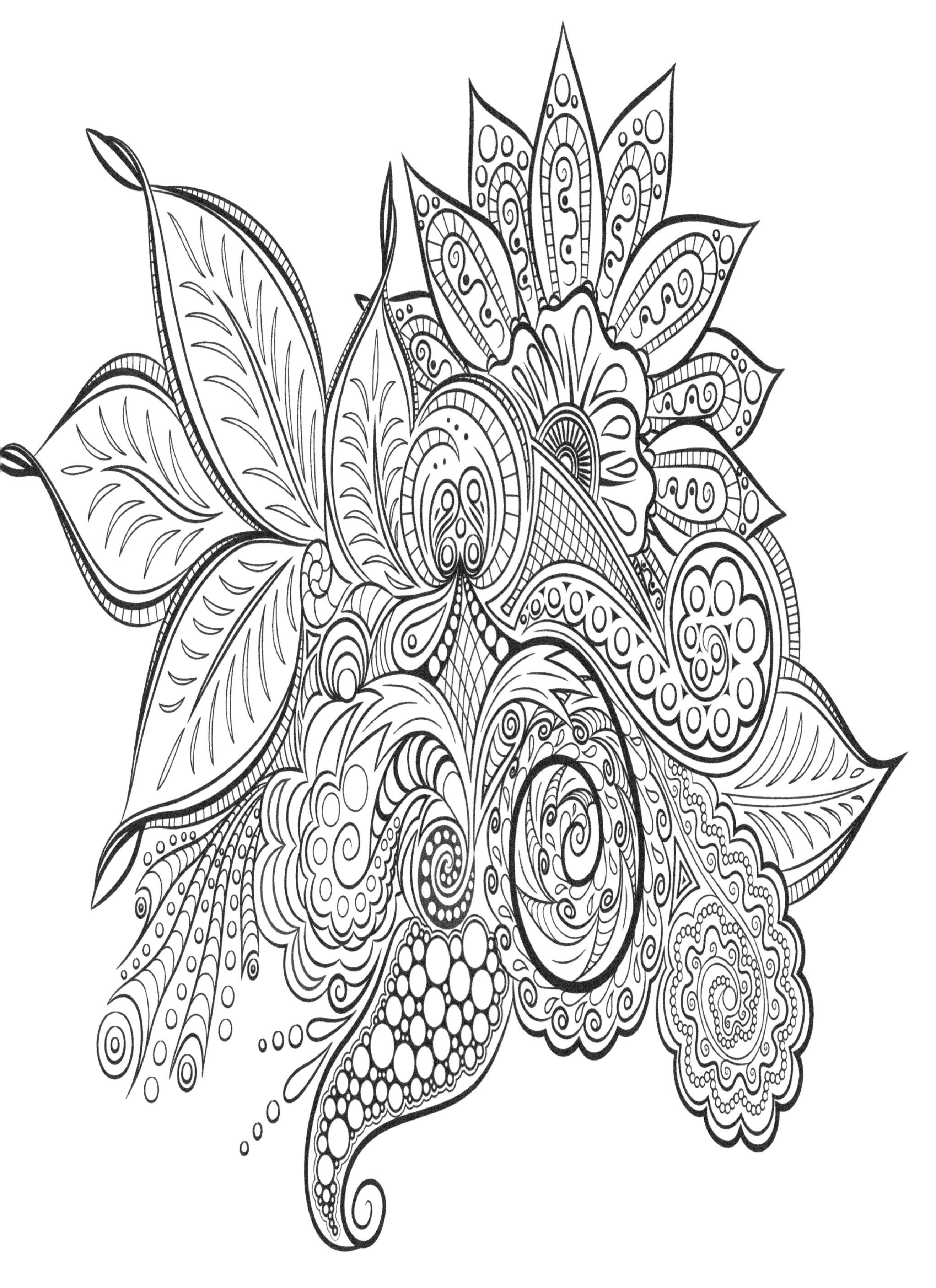

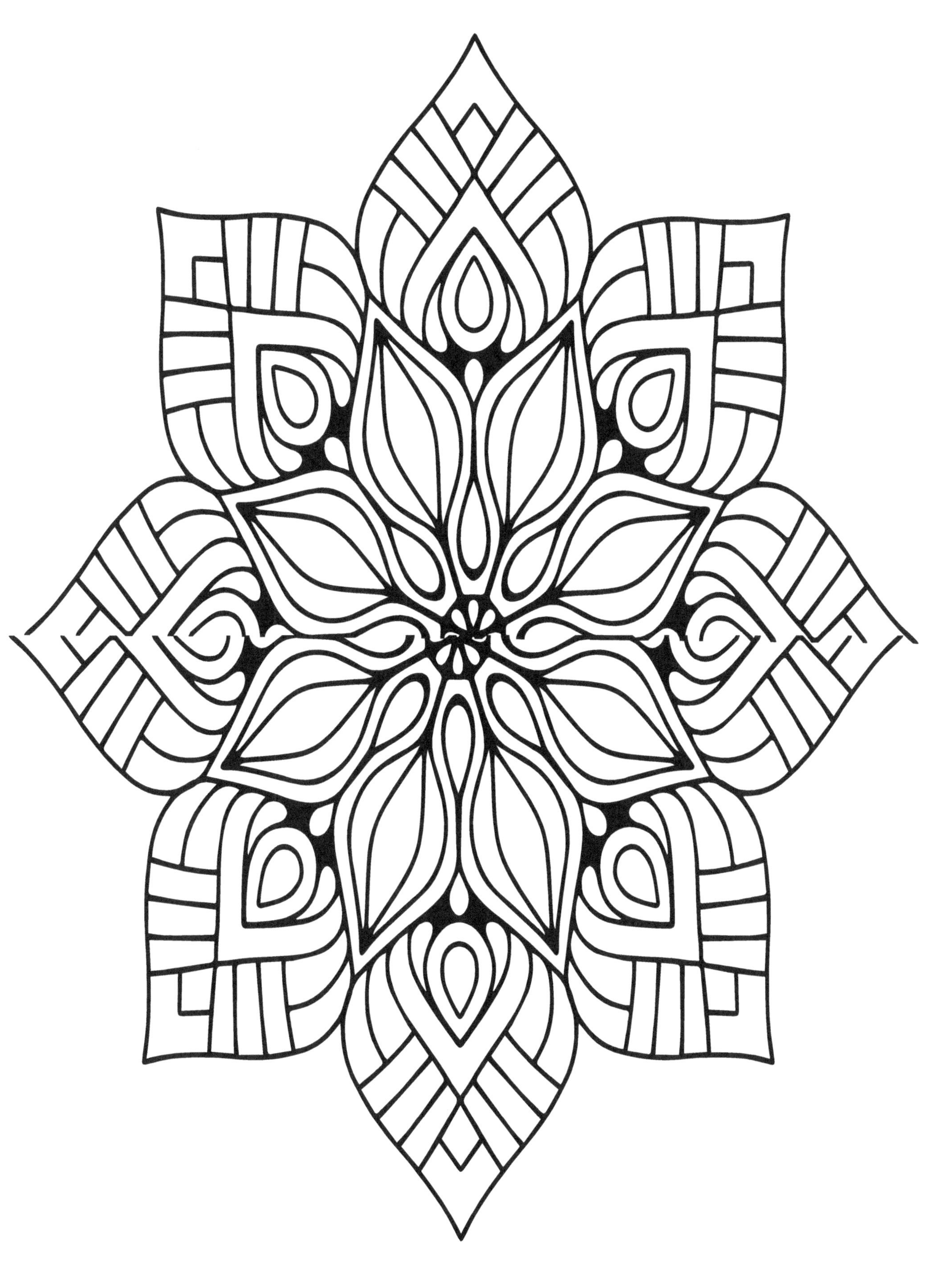

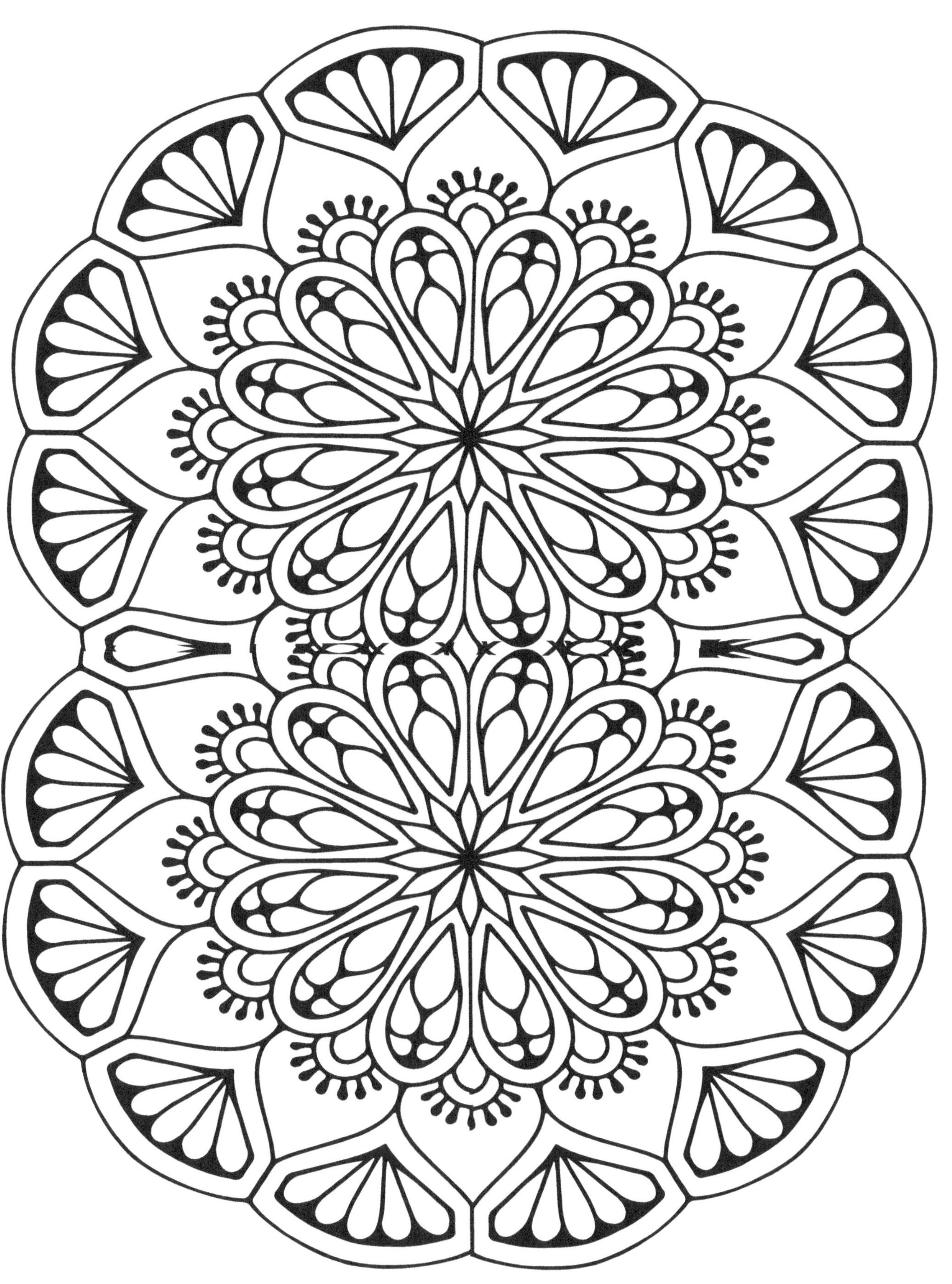

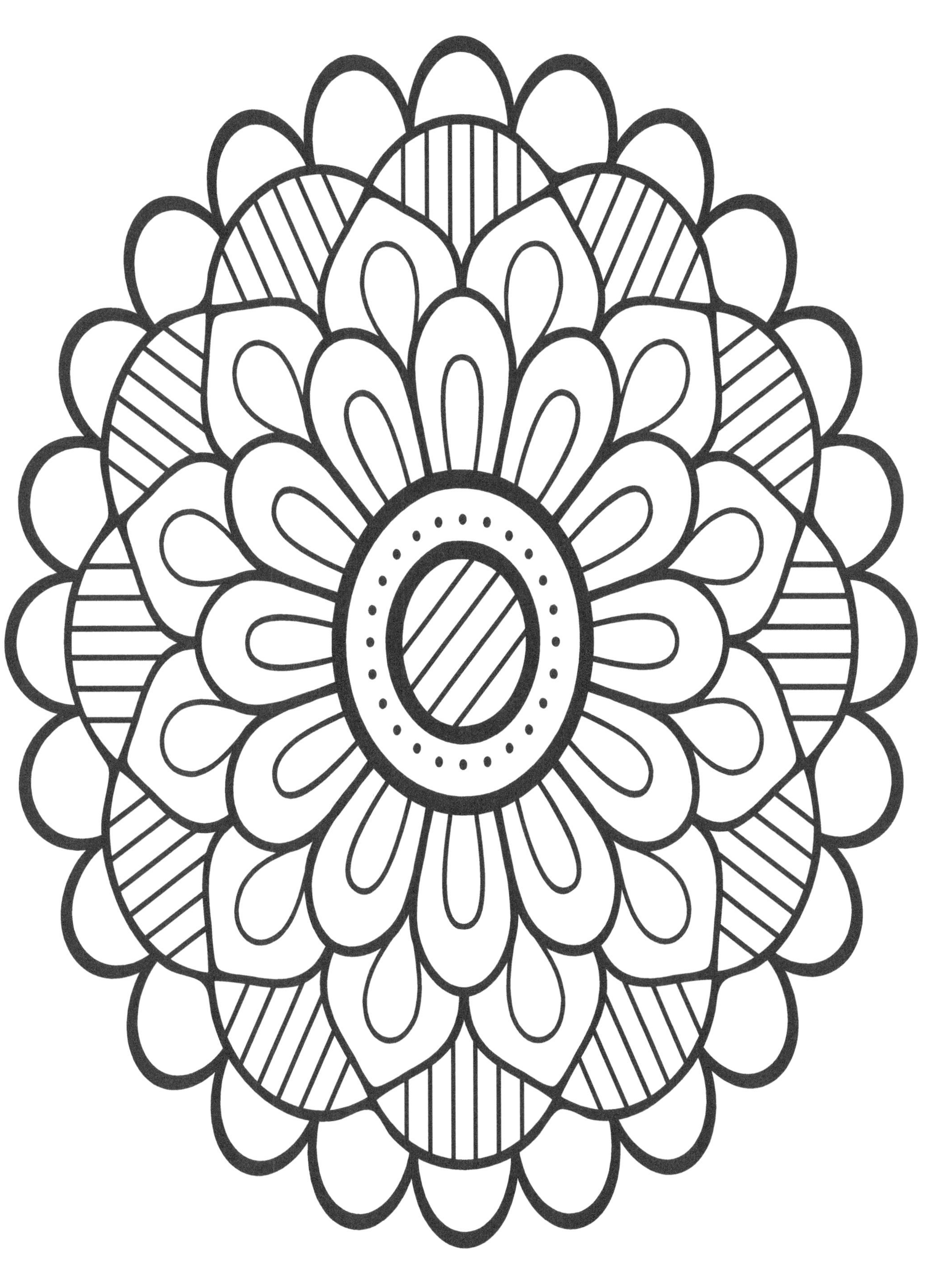

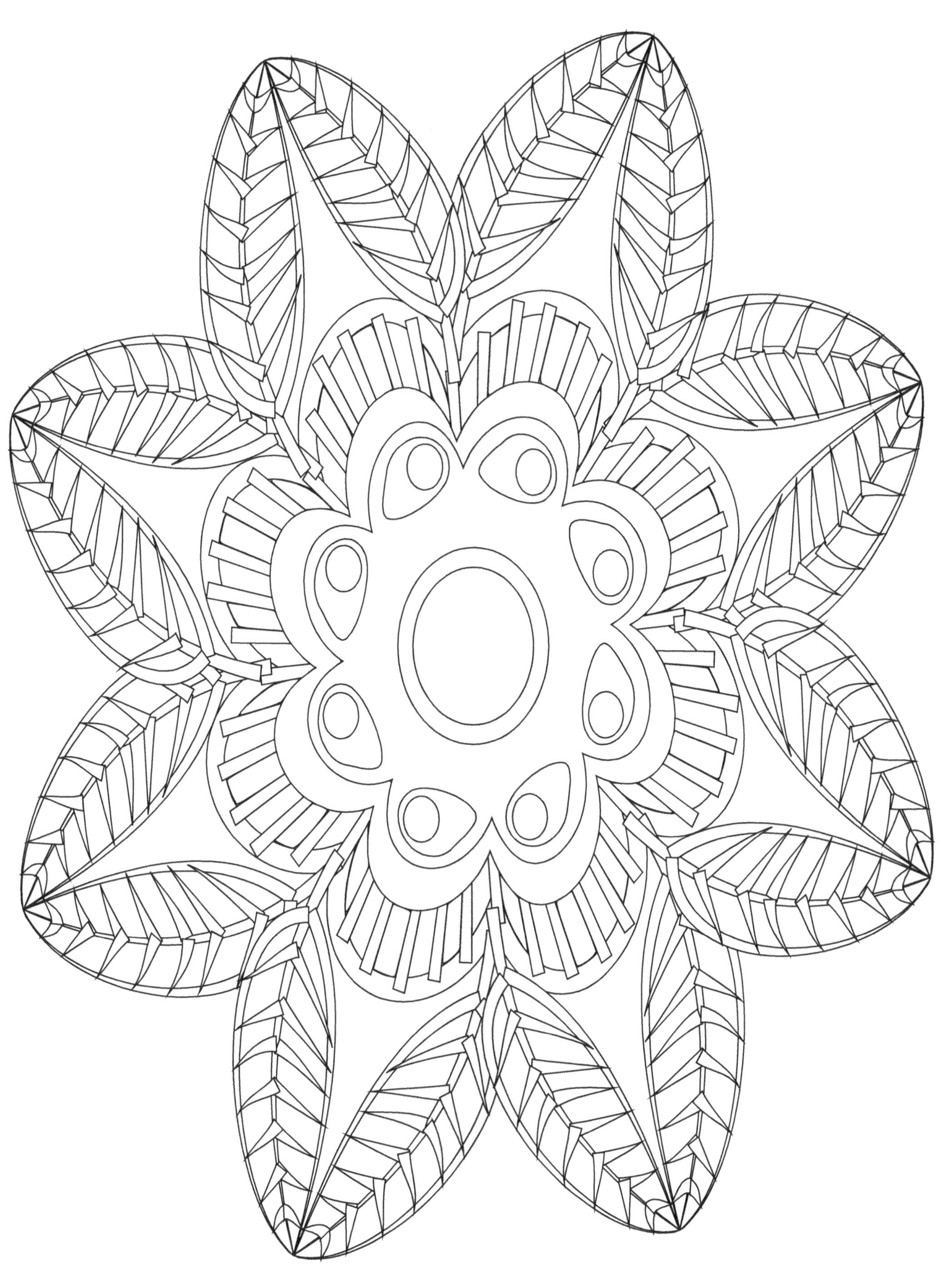

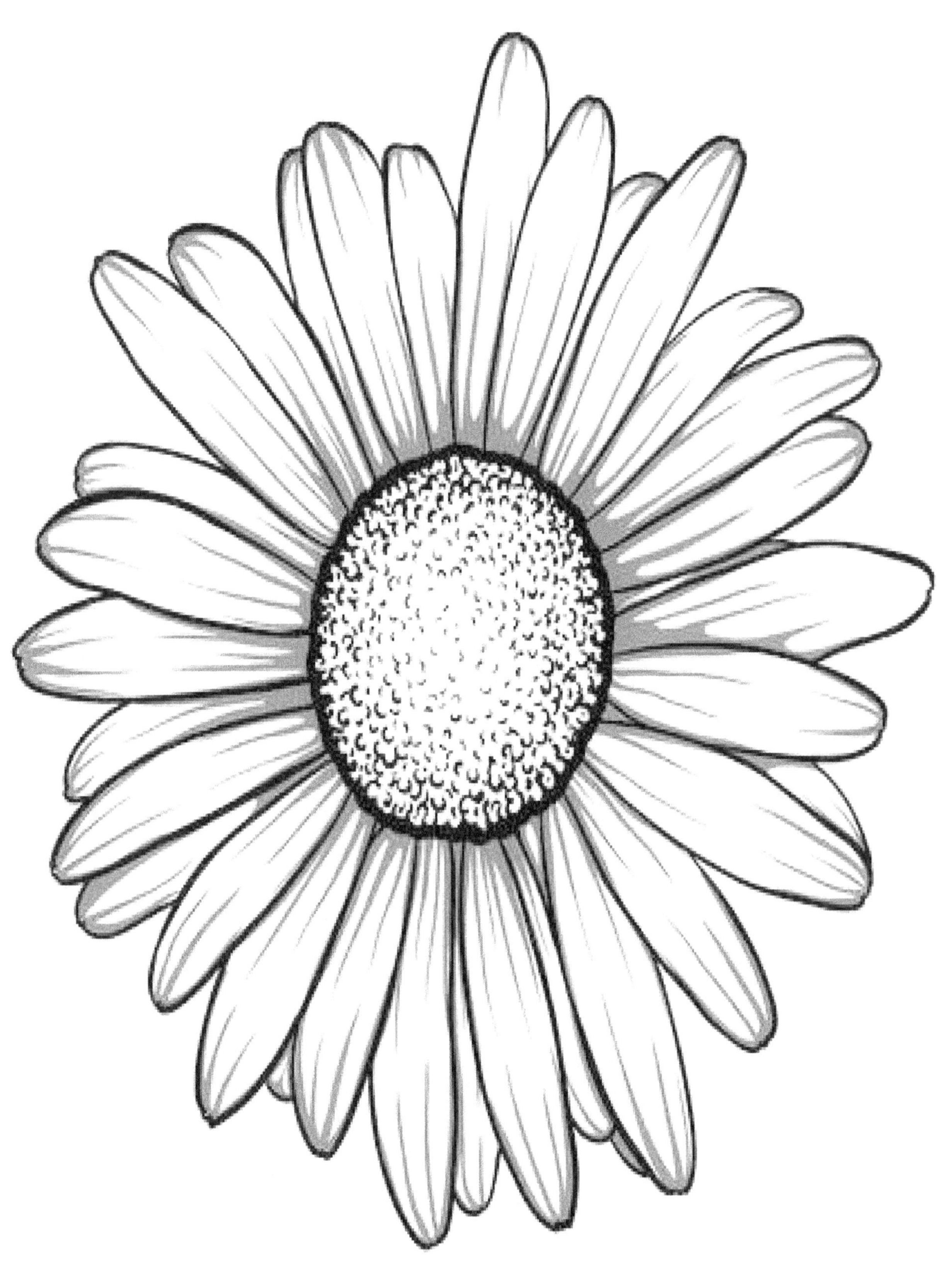

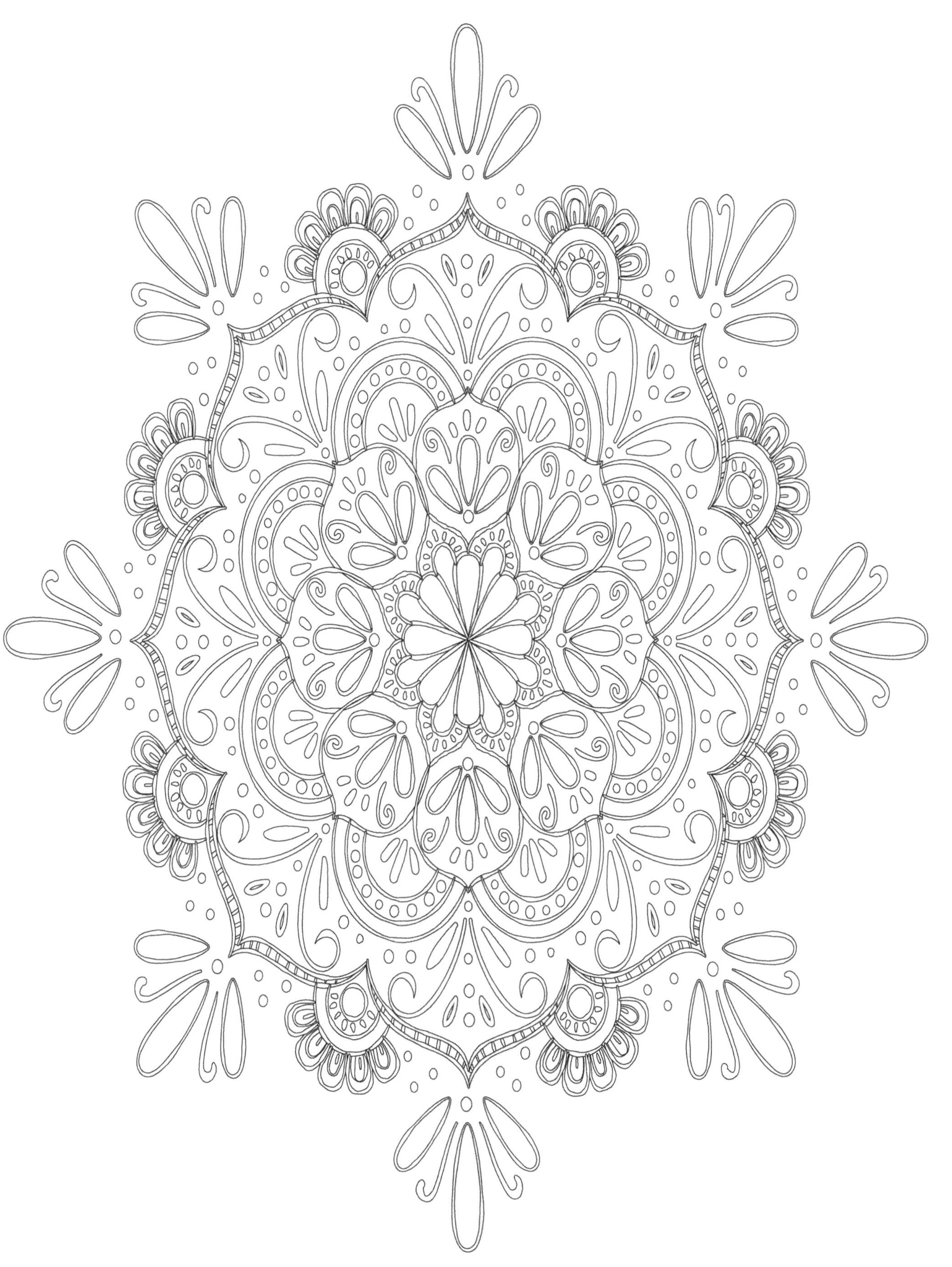

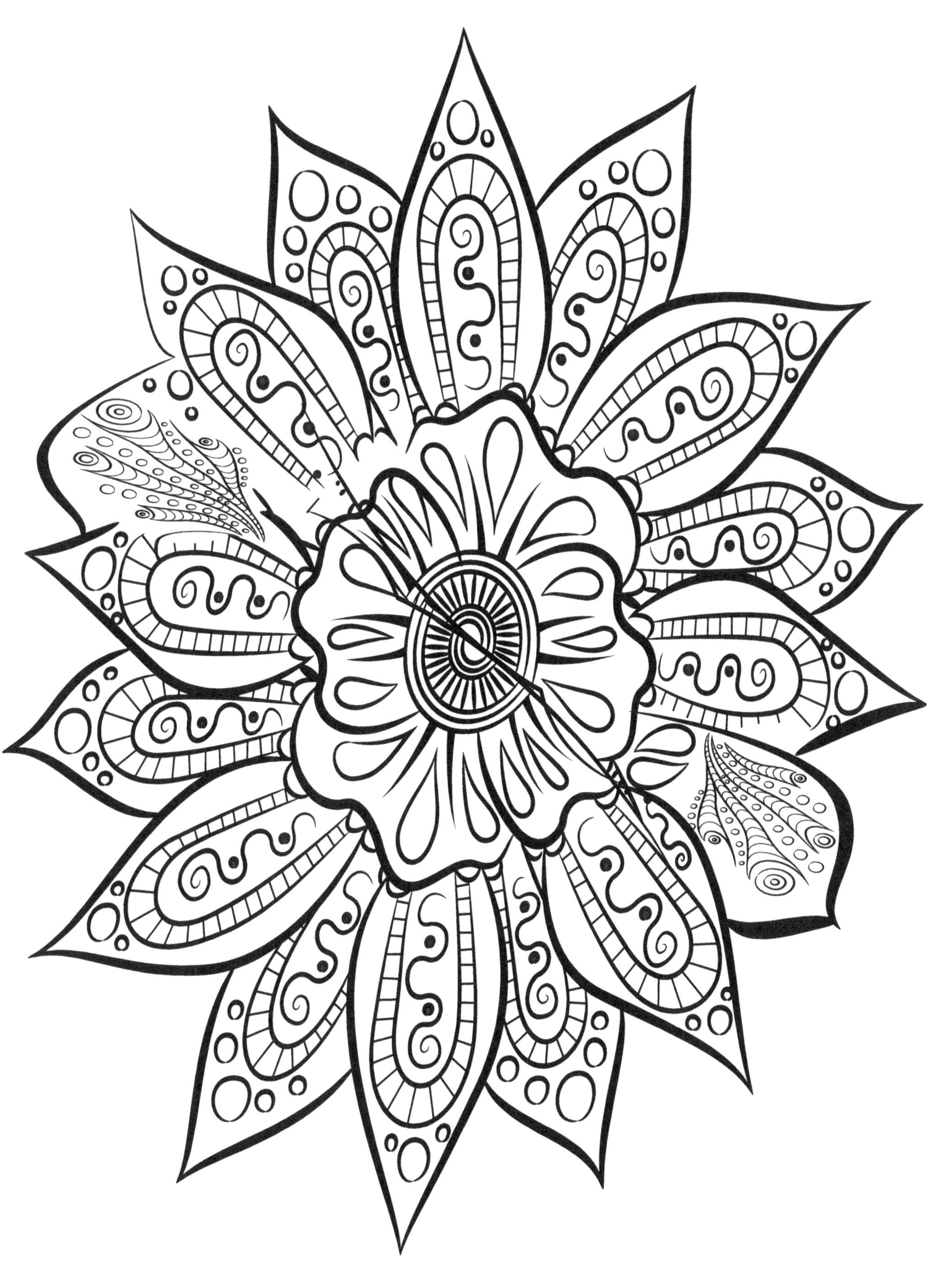

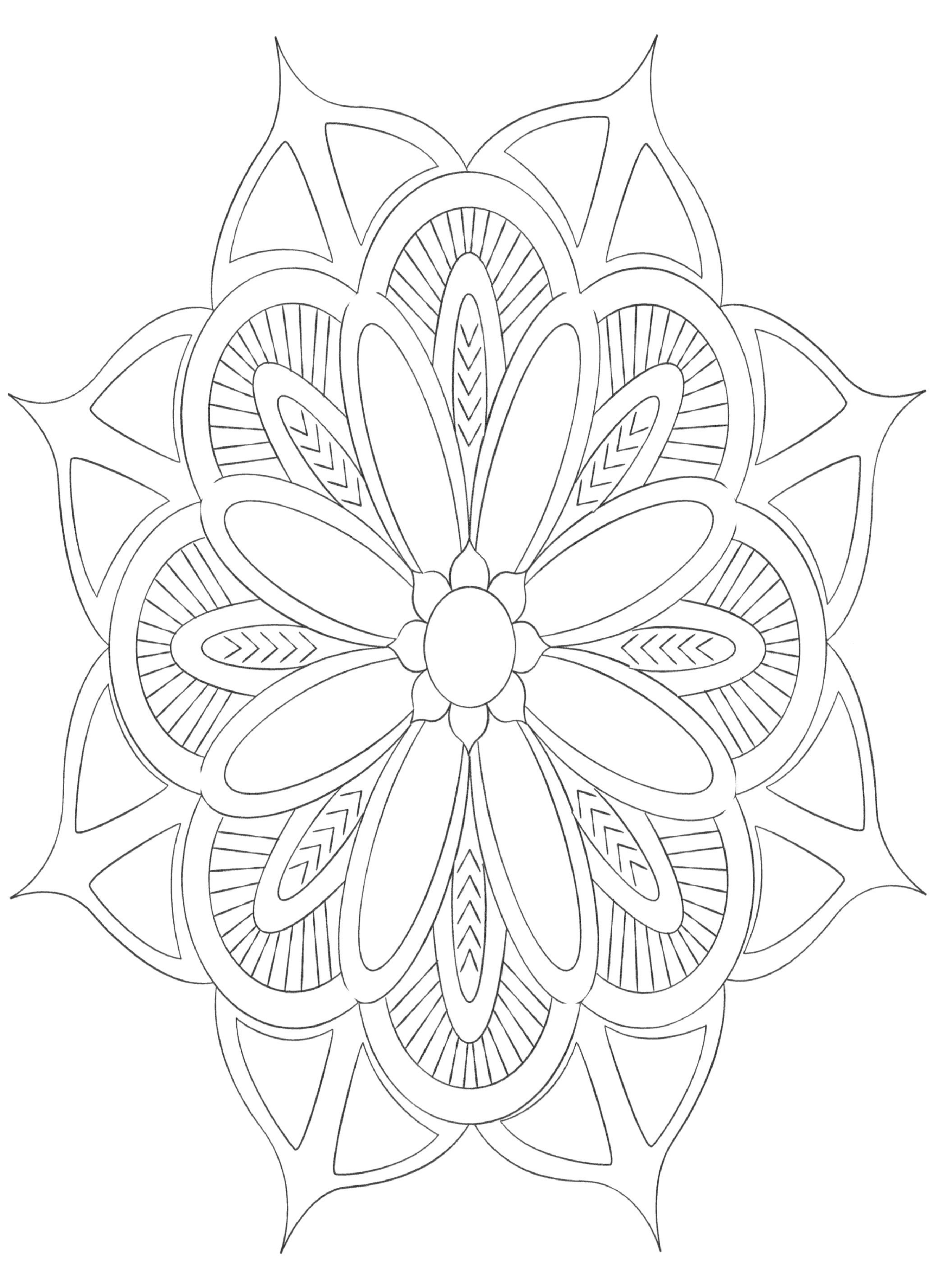

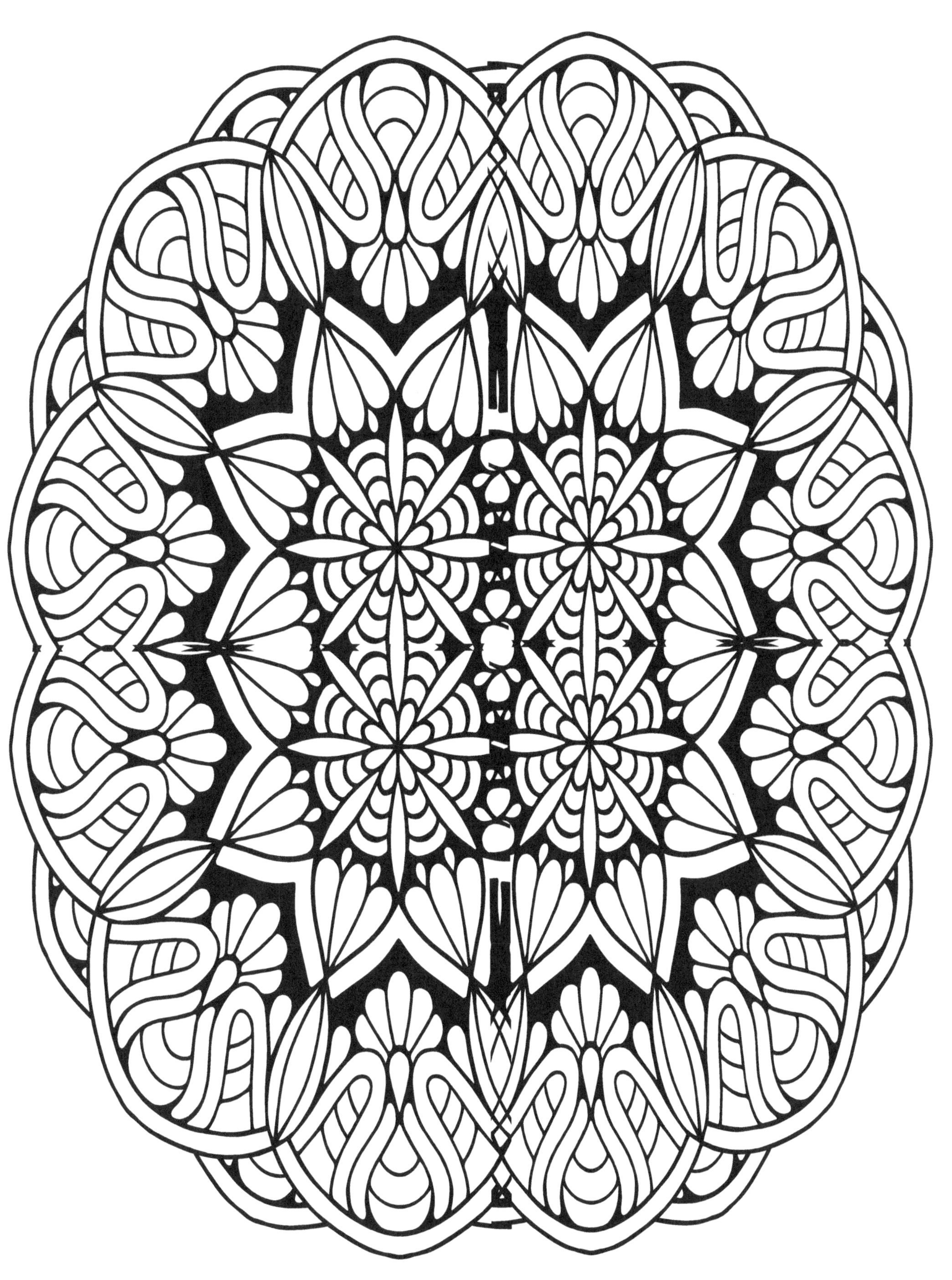

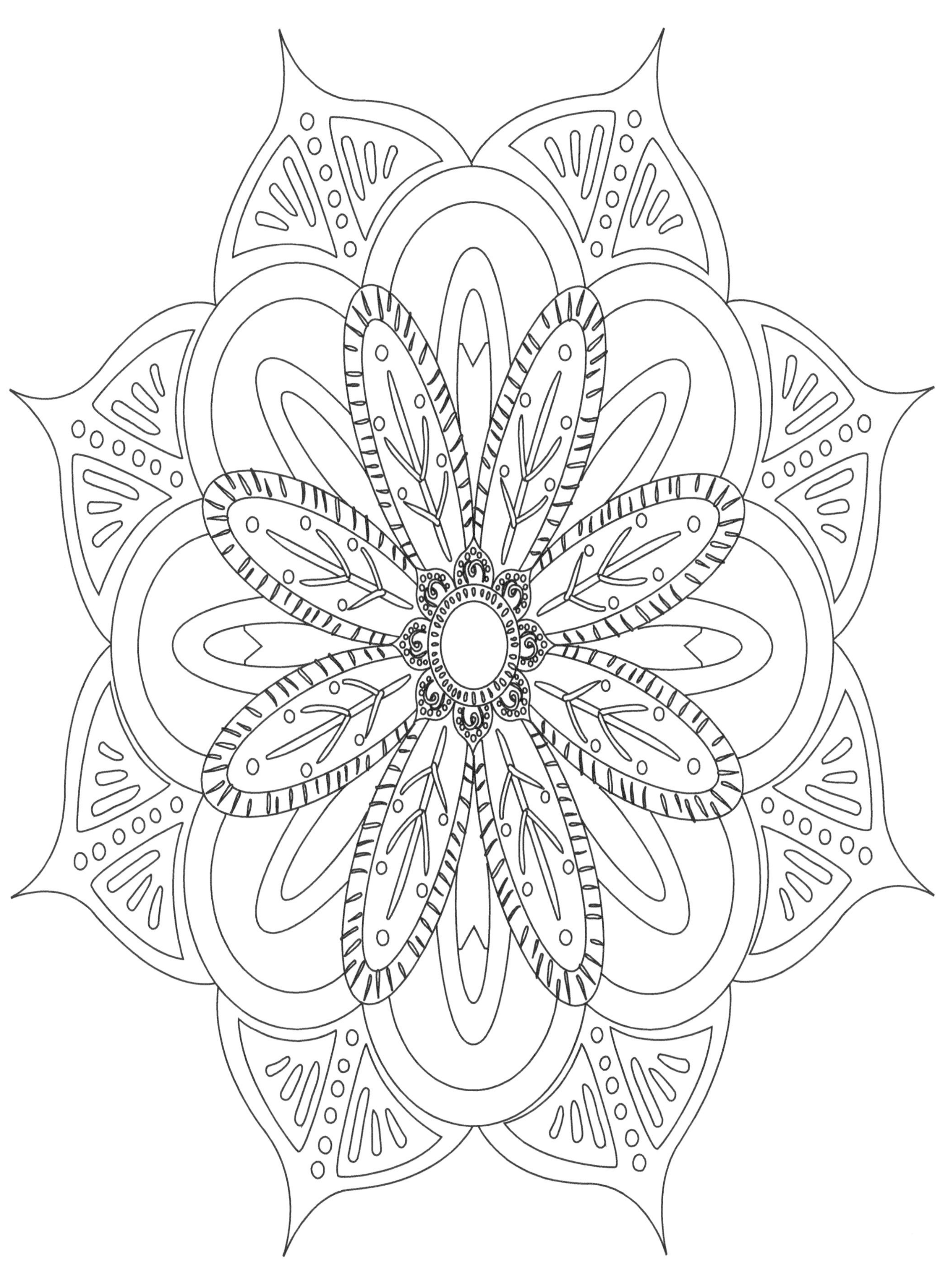

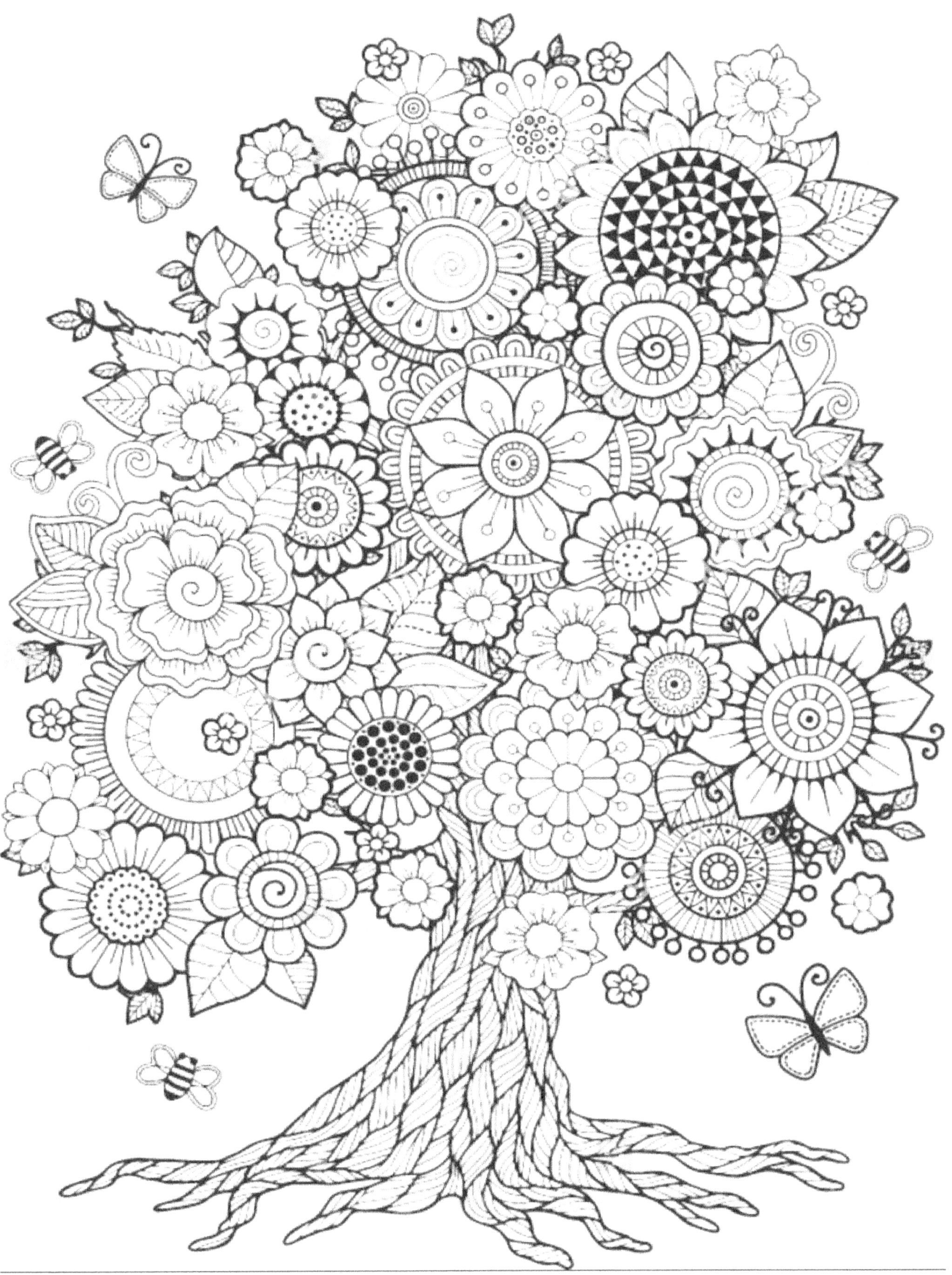

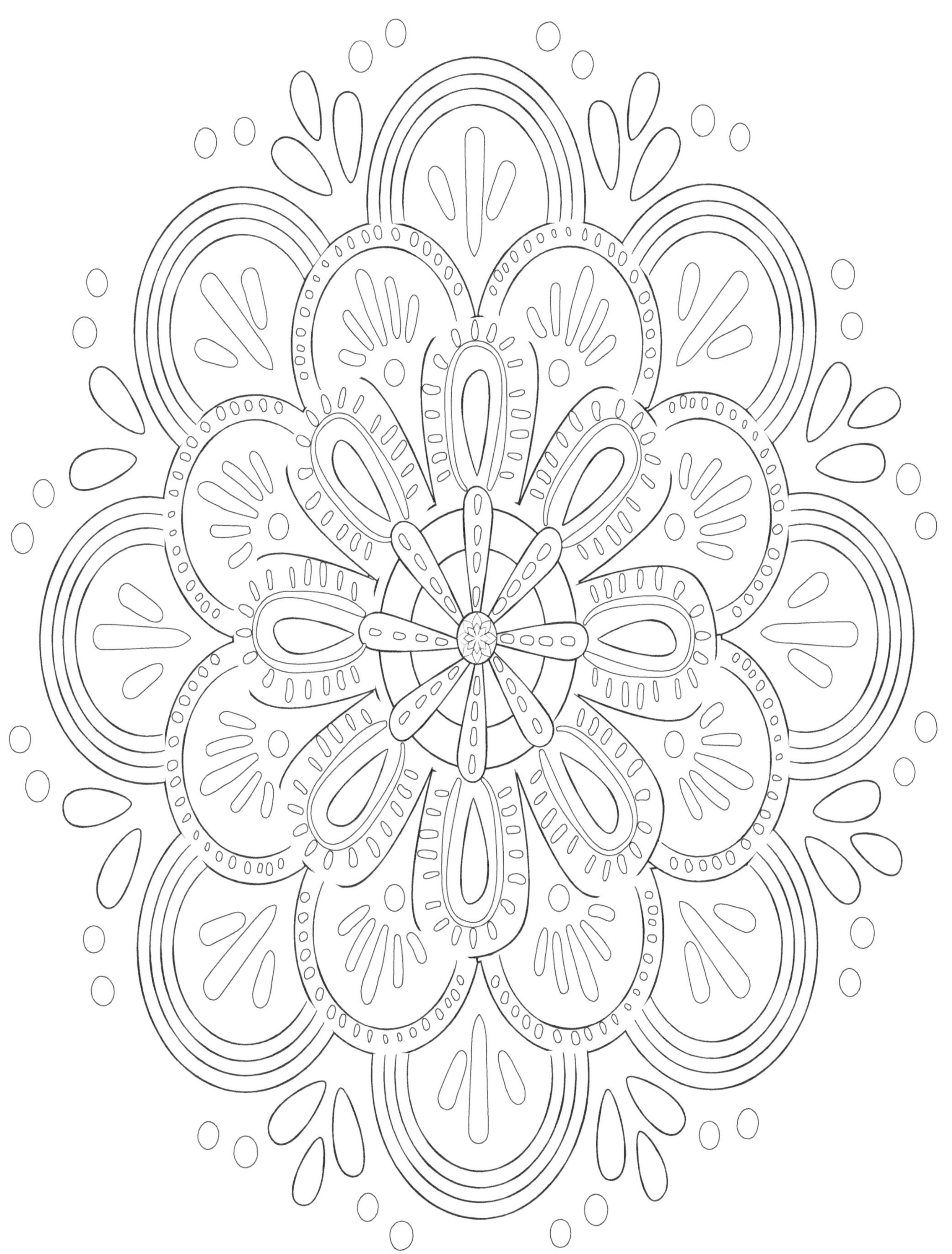

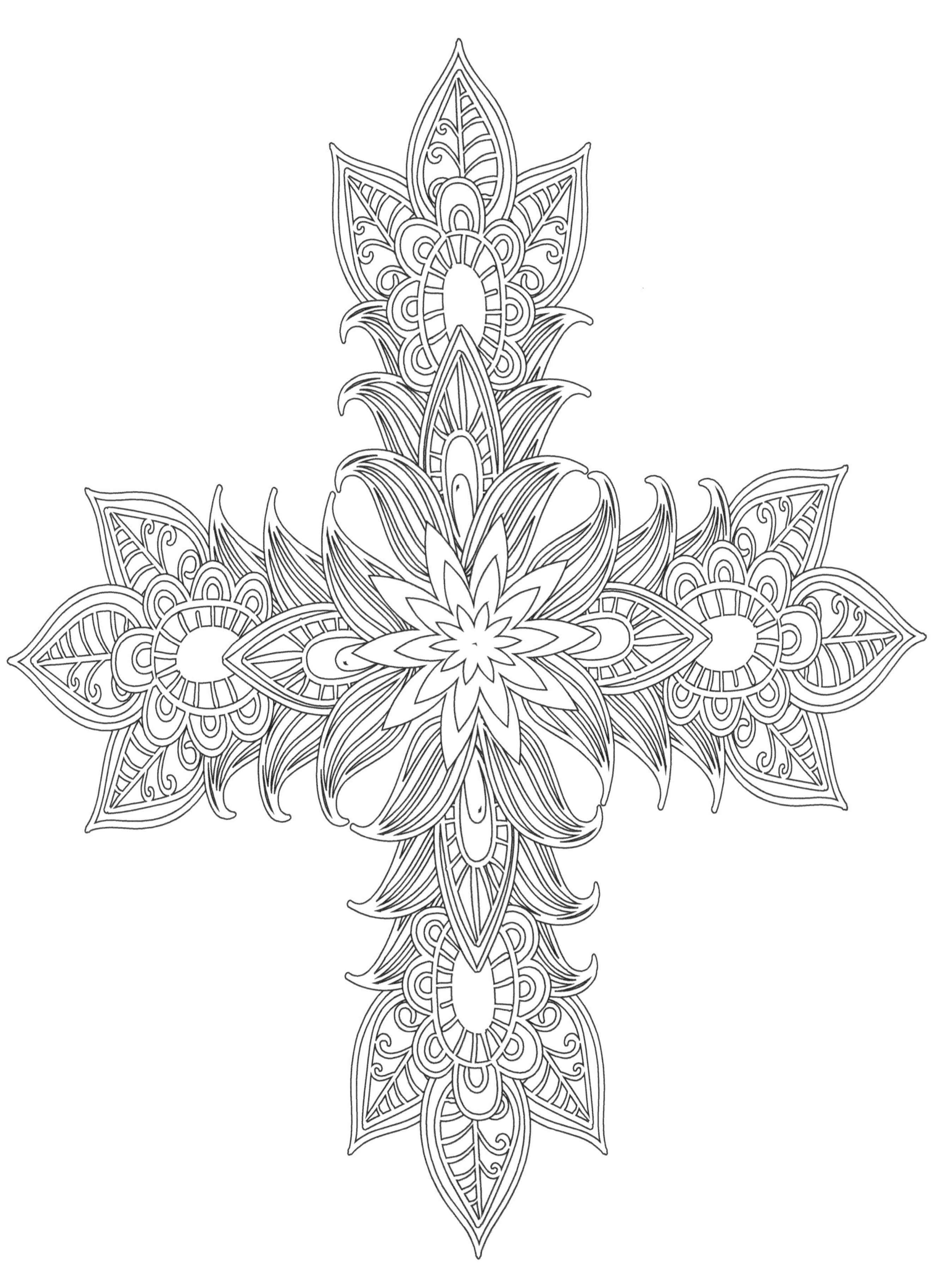

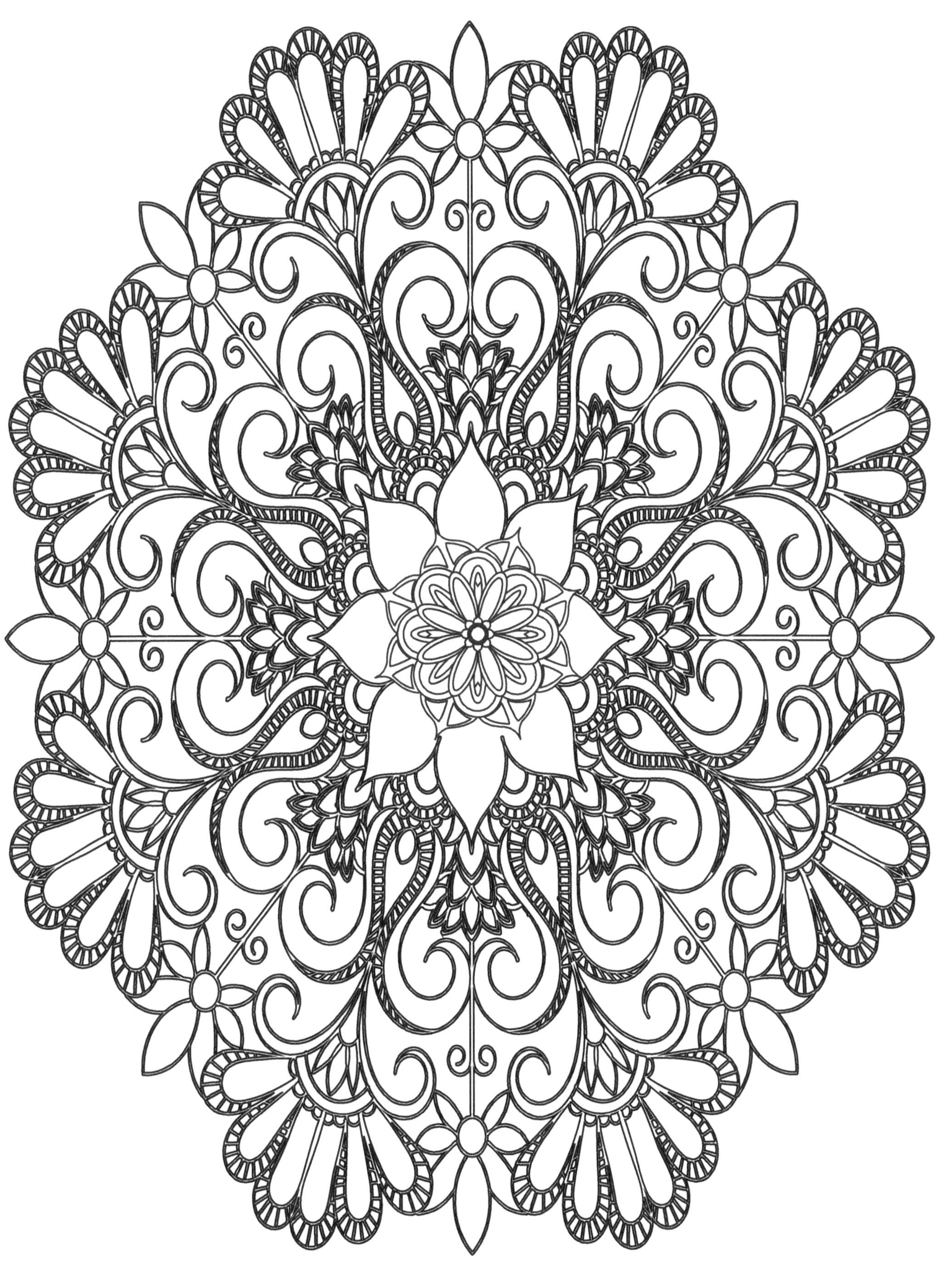

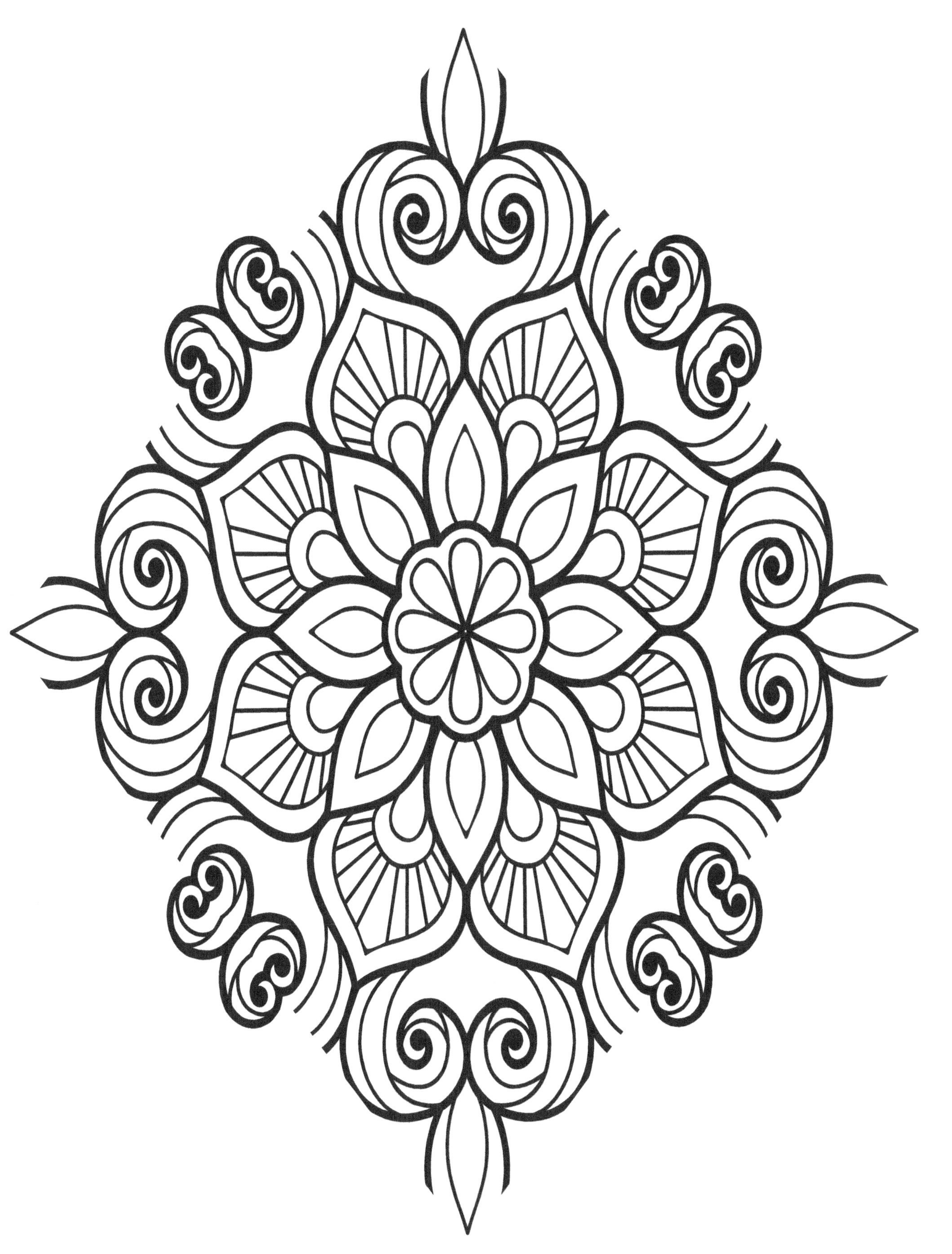

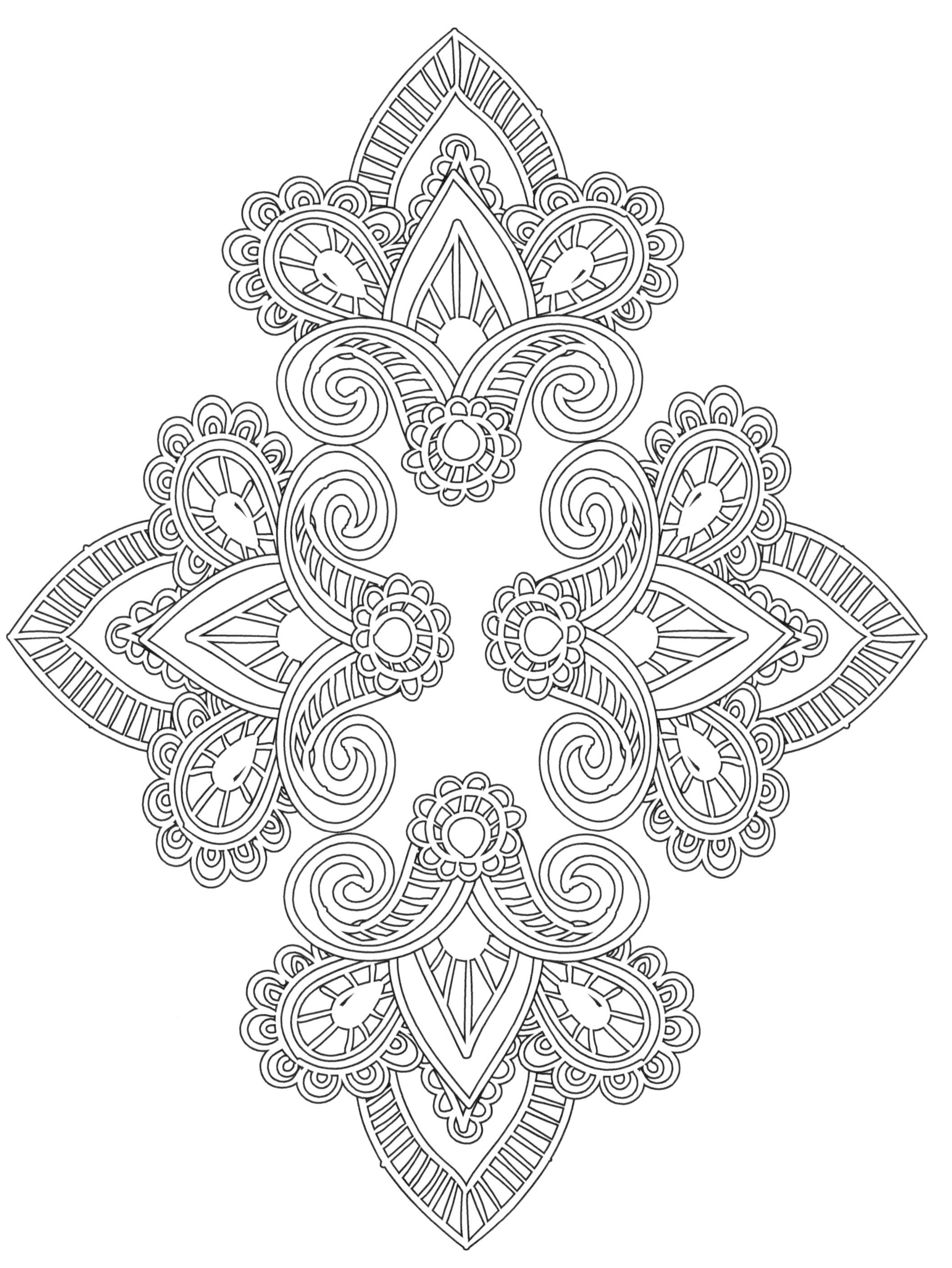

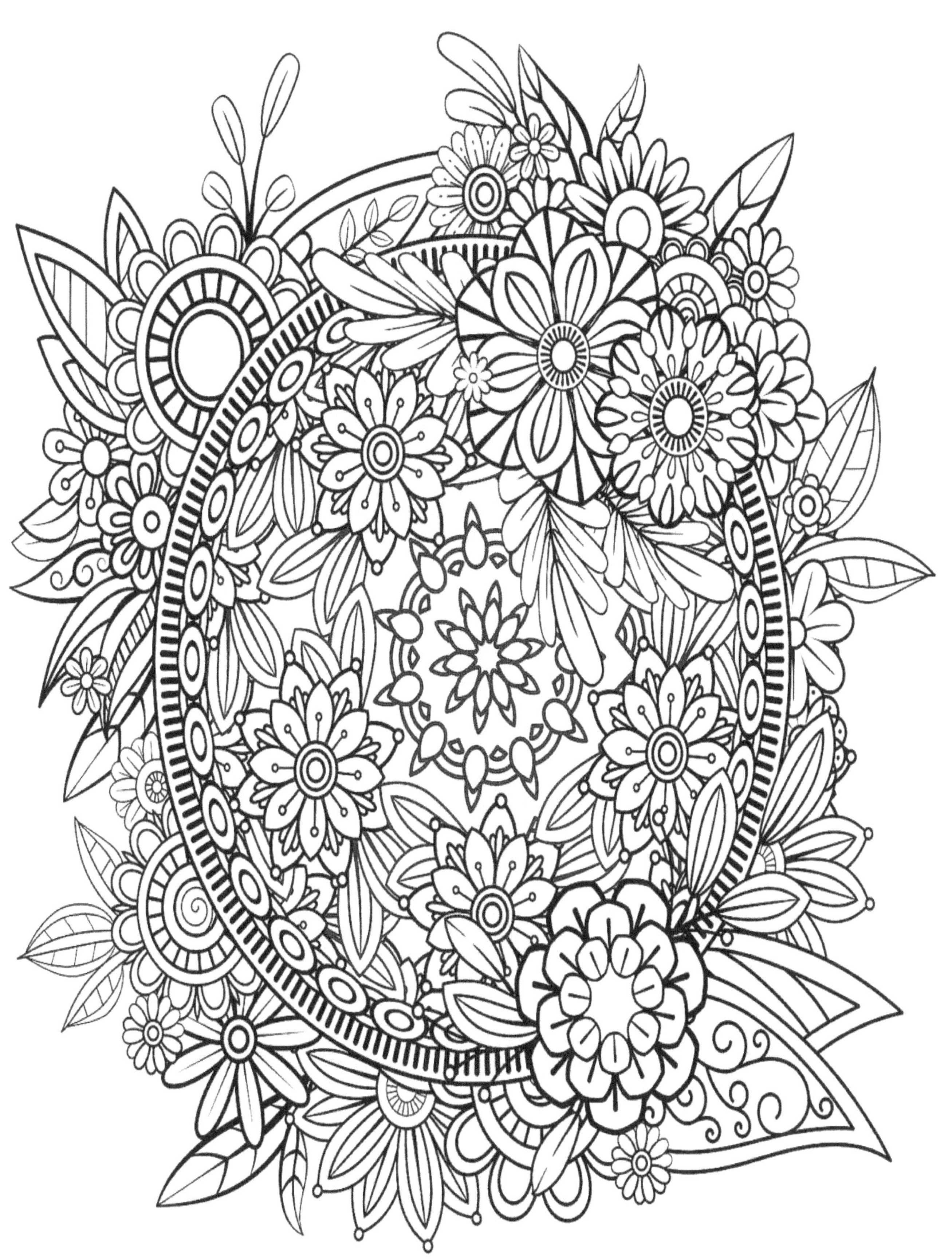

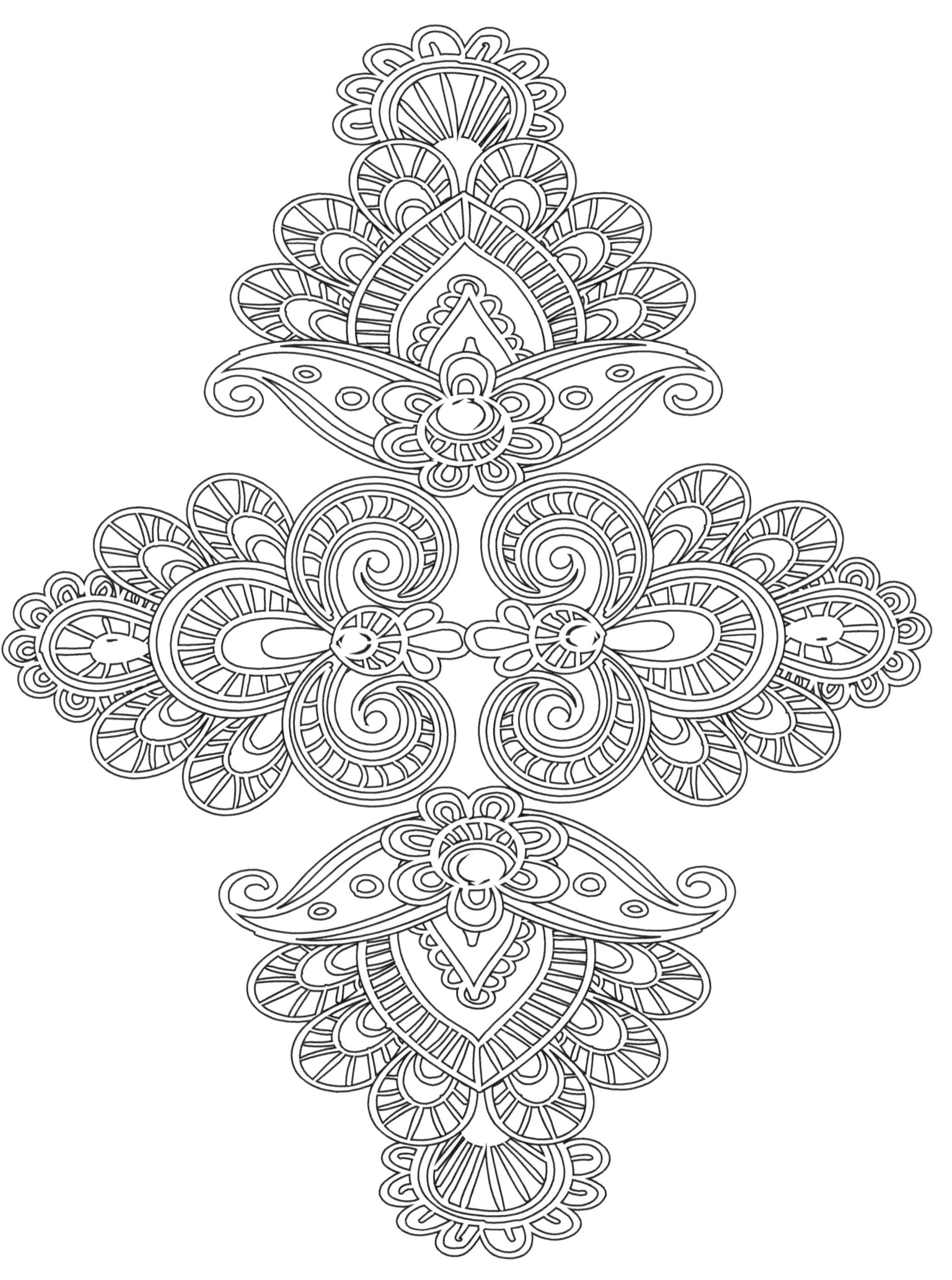

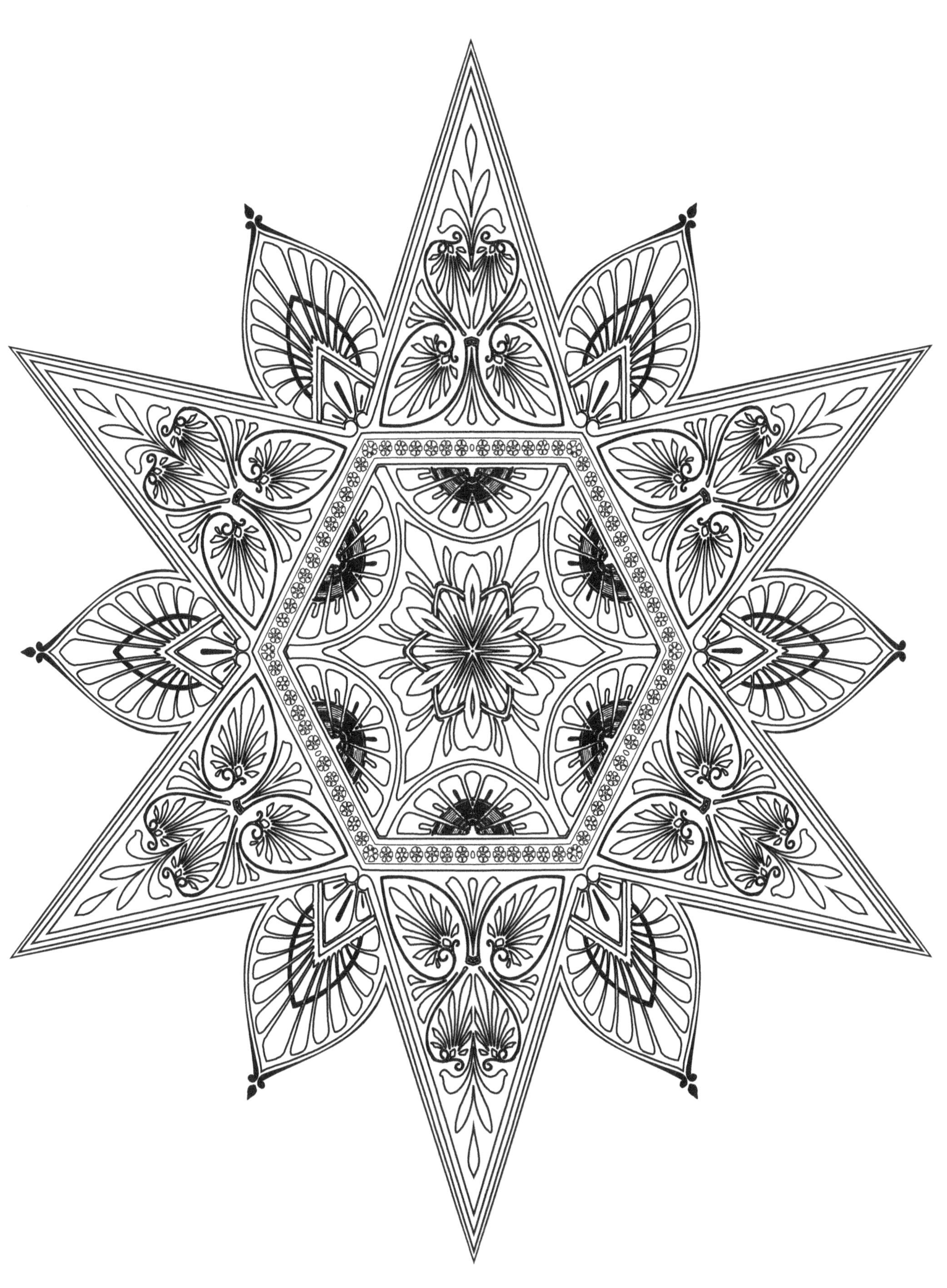

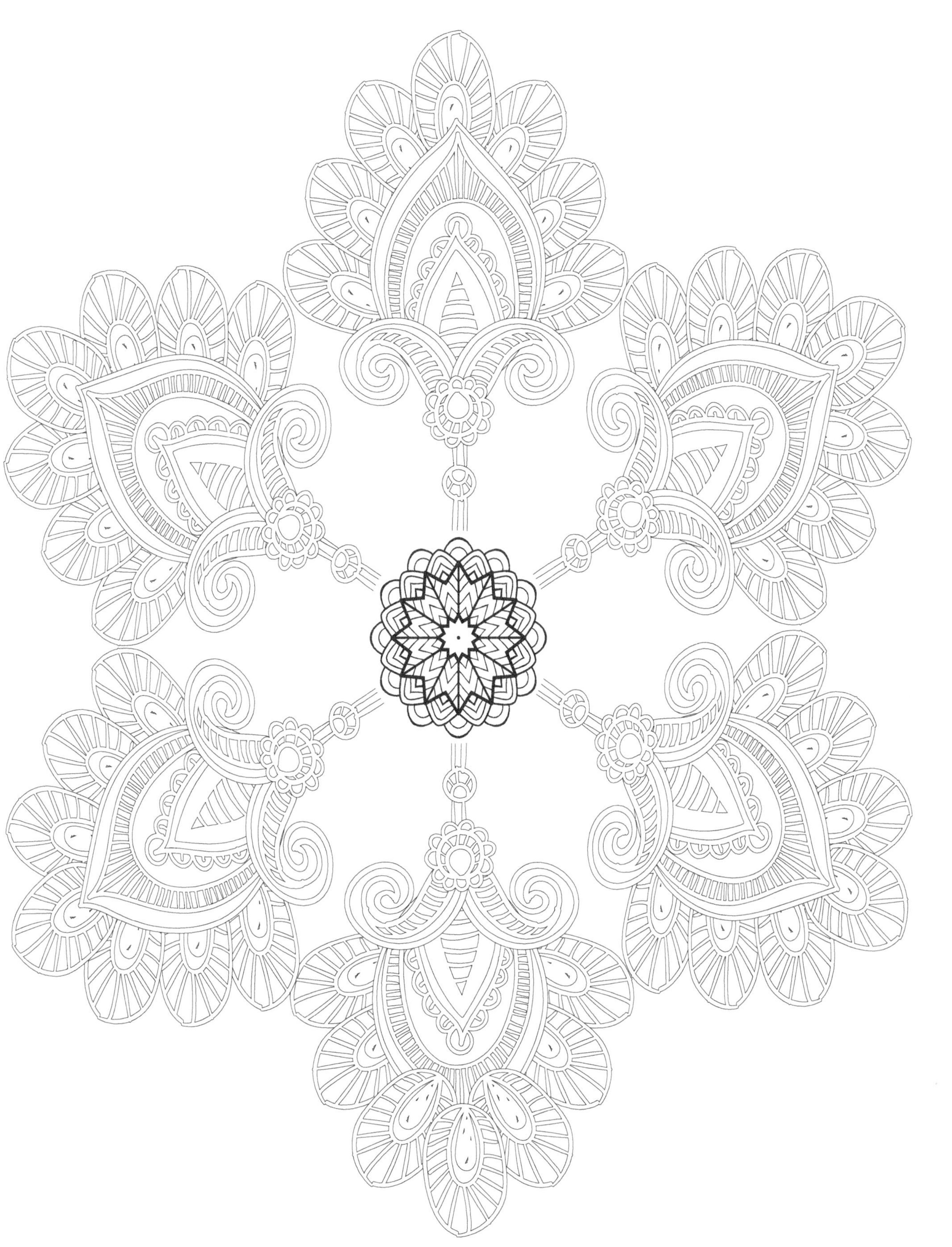

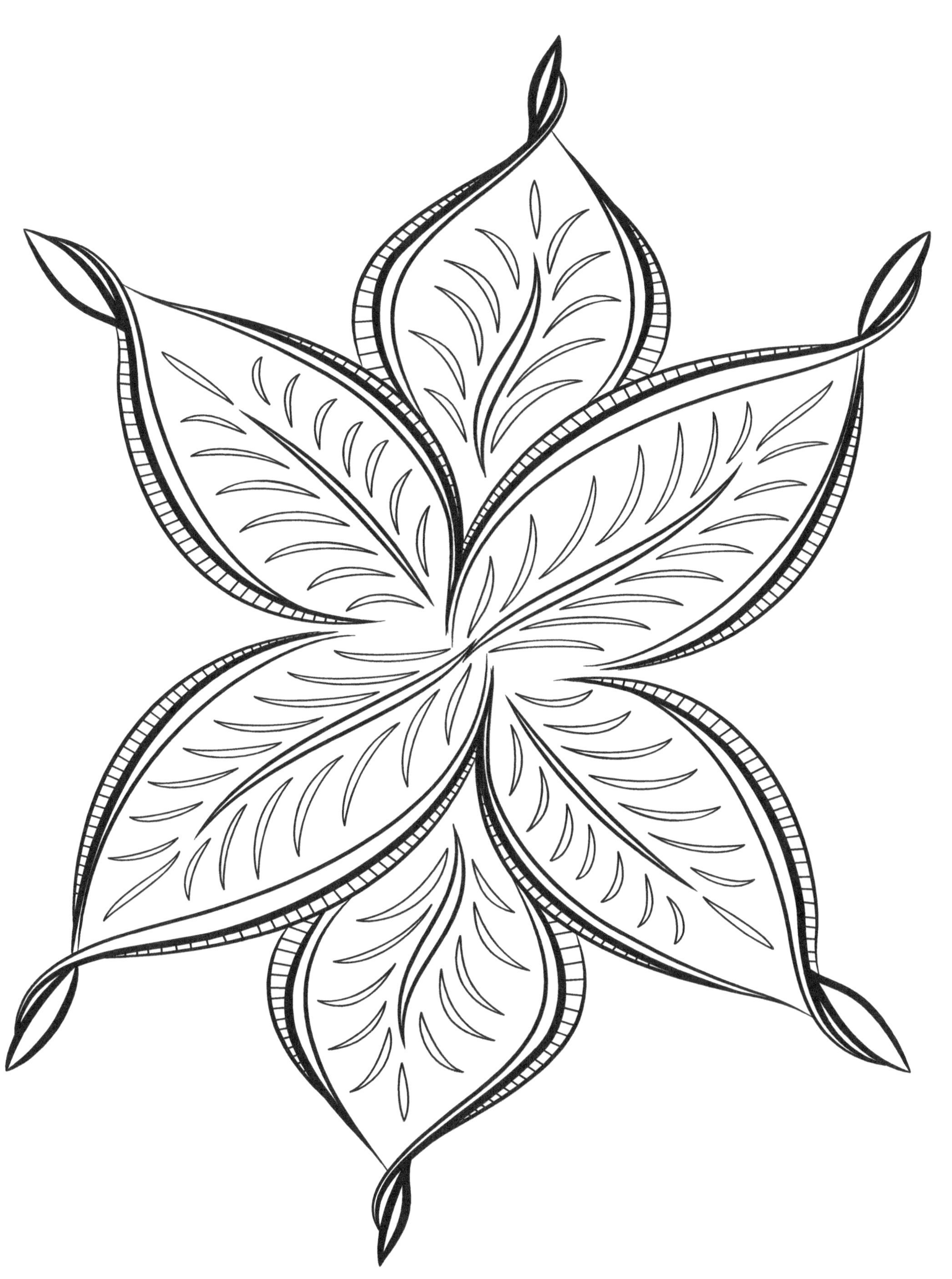

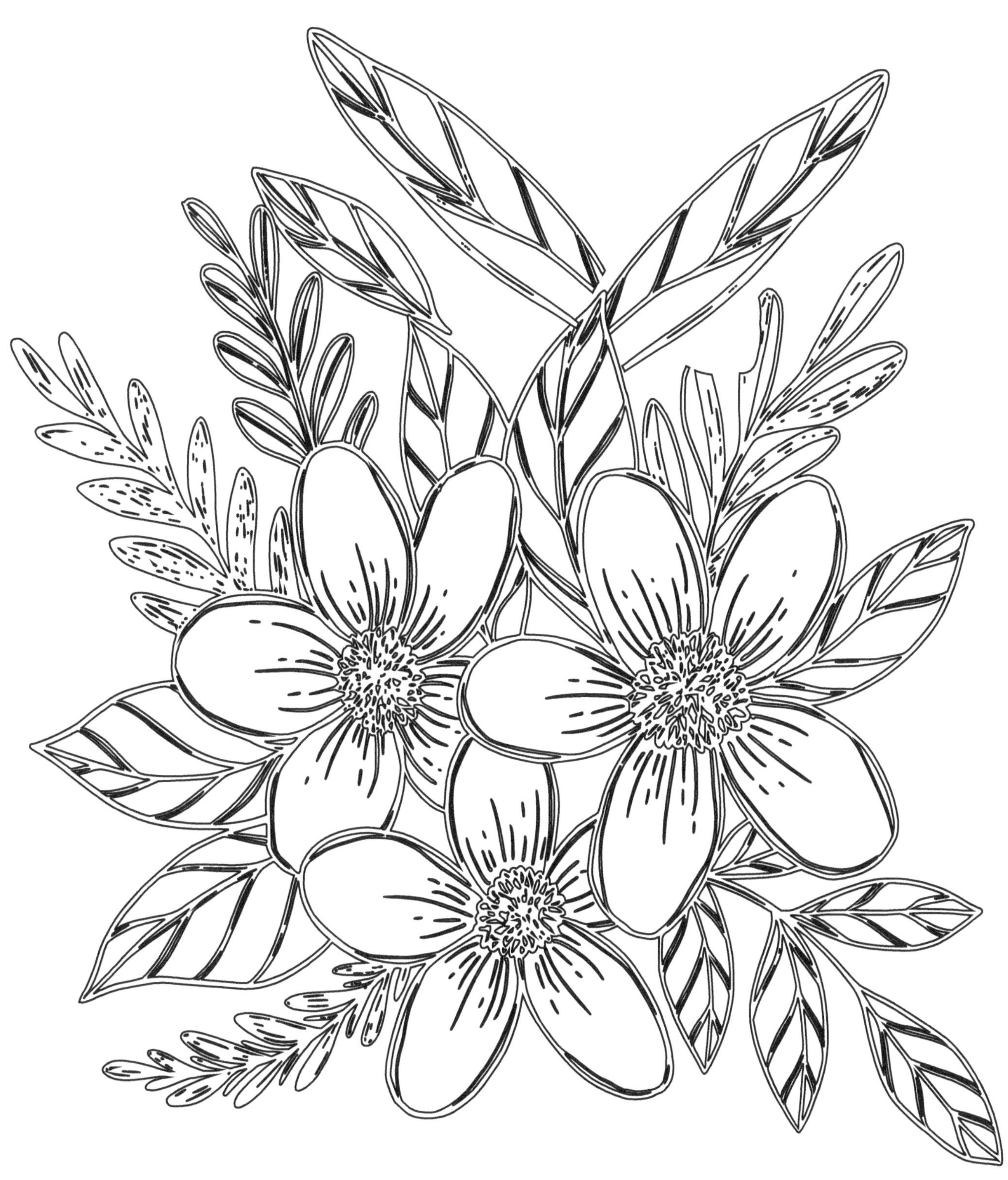